2015 CreateSpace paperback edition
 All rights reserved/First Edition
Published in the United States by Larry A. Frenette
Originally published in paperback cover in the United States by Larry A. Frenette Publishing, an imprint of the of The Amazon Publishing Group, A division of Amazon Publishing, LLC in 2012
Library of Congress Cataloging–in-Publication Data by Frenette, Larry A.
The Isshinryuist: A Tale of Endurance, by Larry A. Frenette
Printed in the United States of America on acid-free paper
www.theisshinryuist.com / www.createspace.com
Editing and book design is credited to Patty Bazzo

# The Isshinryuist: A Tale of Endurance

## Dedication

I want to recognize some of the influential people that were responsible for bringing The Isshinryuist: A Tale of Endurance to life. Nobody has had a larger role in my studying the art of Isshinryu and introducing me to Mr. Johnson's teachings than Sensei Cotton. To my editor Patty Bazzo that made these words dance into sentences. At times, she felt like my nemesis by slashing and slashing until we ended up with a "good read," for which I am grateful... The other two influences were Jason Gilmore and my son Al. These two have stuck with me since the beginning and after six years they are still here, offering guidance and encouragement. Without them it would have been a longer journey than what it was already. Again, a million thanks!

## Introduction

If I miss a day of training, I notice it.
If I miss two days of training my student notices it.
If I miss three days of training my opponent notices it.

The Isshinryuist is a story about my life and how it shaped my character through decades of training. I would consider it a good read that will make you laugh aloud. You will learn practical methods for training and self-defense too.
I started martial arts training in the spring of 1972. I wanted to learn how to fight because I was tired of my brother and the daily beatings he bestowed upon me. At first, I went to a Korean School which was over an hour away and signed an expensive four month contract. Afterwards, I ended at an Isshinryu School which would end up being my life passion. Afterwards, I studied under a point fighter for the next eight years. The next person I trained under was Sensei Cotton: to whom I refer to as my "True Sensei," let the training begin...

# The Isshinryuist: A Tale Of Endurance

# The Isshinryuist: A Tale of Endurance

## Chapters

### Brothers

When we were kids we had a lot of BB-gun fights. I don't know how Craig, my older brother, became involved, because we didn't want him around us due to his meanness. He hid behind a tree looking to shoot someone with his BB gun. He didn't see me and I shot him from behind in his ear lobe. I knew instantly it hurt him "hooray." Once he realized that I was the one who shot him, he charged towards me. I had one of those Daisy rifles similar to the ones shown on the movie "Christmas Story." He thought I'd be scared and start running or lie down and cry. But he underestimated the fact that I was an incredible shot due to years of practice, comparable to the way I can work a Bo (staff) in martial arts. Though I was scared, I never got my butt kicked without fighting back. I had excellent cover, a big maple tree with forty feet between us. Craig covered ten feet before I knew what was happening. I pumped ten shots into him within the next five feet and another five upon his retreat. When he made it back to his tree, he started his habitual yelling, "I'm going to beat you up!" Maybe so, I thought, but it's not going to happen today. I hid behind the maple tree and laughed hysterically and felt proud of my deed. Nevertheless, I knew that in the end I would pay and he would bury his knuckles in to my flesh. I don't ever remember playing or hanging around with Craig. I always kept my distance and stacked the odds in my favor by leaving the house before anyone was up.

I had another brother, Gary. He was a normal brother who beat on me now and then, but in a playful manner. Gary was a brave soul and one of the craftiest people you could ever meet. Gary and Craig fought often and on rare occasions Gary stuck up for me, and in doing so he got hurt. However, it was never an outright win for Craig. Gary fought until the end, though he preferred the hit-and-run method. Sometimes he slugged Craig in the head and took off running, which infuriated Craig. Gary ran about fifteen feet in front of Craig and kept this distance throughout the pursuit. During the next hour and a half they passed us several times while running around our block, which was a mile and a half in length. The whole neighborhood was intrigued at this event, which was a common occurrence. Gary always lost Craig. Craig came home to wait for Gary by the bushes near the front door. Beforehand, he locked the basement door, leaving only one entrance accessible. The fight lasted all day. Gary never came home until it got dark. Craig knew that if Gary made it inside the house mom would save him. Gary made his move and got inside the house before Craig could get a hold of him and Gary used mom as a shield. The whole house was in turmoil. Gary knew exactly where mom would be and he slammed the door on Craig as he came in. Craig didn't punch him for fear of hitting mom and involving dad. I sat on the couch watching TV waiting for this treasured moment. Mom yelled at Craig demanding that he leave Gary alone; otherwise, she threatened to tell dad. Gary, on the other hand, punched Craig in the head a couple of times, which really heated things up. I loved watching this family feud.

Once, Gary beat me up then he laid against a tree for a siesta. I took a shovel and dug a waist-deep hole on a wooded path that led us around to Uncle Santini's house. After I finished digging the hole, I put twigs across it and crisscrossed them in a way where they were spaced close enough together to hold the leaves that covered up the two-and-a-half foot diameter hole. I thrust a stick in the ground next to the path as a reference point to let me know when to jump (I had devised a hell of a plan). Gary was still asleep. I grabbed a stick about six inches long and threw it at him hitting him directly in the face. He was angry and started running after me. He was about three feet behind me when his life was about to change. I jumped at my reference point; Gary let out a scream and when I turned around, he had one leg in the hole and the other leg out of the hole. He looked like a hurdler in an outstretched position and crying. For hours I heard dad yelling out for me. He later scolded me for not coming home when I heard him yell out my name. Coming home would have meant a beating and two weeks of punishment in the yard. Some people call this "thinking out of the box." I call it "thinking outside of the hole…"

Rowe Lake was the main attraction in our neighborhood through all seasons where we fished, swam, skated and played hockey. Everyone in the neighborhood congregated near the lake. The nice thing about Rowe Lake was weren't any motor boats, so there was no oily film floating on top of the water like most lakes. While skating, Craig slapped me and then he fell down. I kicked him in the head with my figure skates. I knew for certain that this was a win. His head was bleeding, but he got up and beat me up. For me to outright attack him, he had to do something bad. Craig never let me have a good time.

# The Isshinryuist: A Tale of Endurance

When Gary bar-brawled, he threw pool balls, this was an effective self-defense. Gary seemed to have a black cloud following him. While he was working in a little factory in Sterling Heights, something heavy fell on his back; when he looked up to see what it was, something else fell and broke his nose. He had his nose broken so many times that if you stood at his side, it appeared as if he were looking at you. Gary was always in trouble because he had the balls of a rhinoceros. He did all kinds of drugs, including heroin. When he lived in Mt. Clemens, he told me that his place had been broken into and that most of his stuff was stolen. He knew who did it because he hung with this crowd. He got his revenge by putting an ax through the front window of the house, but he never caught anyone because everyone scattered out the back door. Later, he accosted one of the men on the sidewalk knowing that he carried a knife. Gary thought he could get him before he pulled it out. Again, that black cloud was hovering above him. The blade caught him in the middle of his cheek stopping just short of his tear duct. I visited him in the emergency room with mom and dad. I tried to make him feel better by pointing out that at least they didn't get his nose. Because of the car accidents, the fights and the other incidents I didn't think his nose could have taken another hit. After he recovered, he was driving around Mt. Clemens when he saw the man who cut him. Gary then drove his car onto the sidewalk. The man started running to get out of harm's way, but he wasn't fast enough for the brown, LTD Crowne Victoria. After he ran him over, he just drove to Florida and started working on shrimp boats.

The last time I saw him was when he visited us for Christmas; he died the following year. I never sparred with him, but on his last visit he attacked me in the kitchen. And to his amazement, I delivered a lunge-punch to his ribs that penetrated his dress-leather, which caused him to back off. After this, he gave up on the idea of dominating me as he had done in the past.

I miss Gary. He was a fun guy who met his fate too early. He was stabbed through the heart by a man whom he had just beaten up in a bar. After doing so, Gary stayed in the bar drinking beer. The man came back later with a buck-knife looking for revenge and stabbed him in the heart. (I teach that after an altercation you should leave. The first thing you need to know about self-defense is that you must try to get yourself out of the situation peacefully, if at all possible. If you do have to fight, fight as though you are putting your attacker away before he can get his knife out).

## Craig

Craig is the reason why I turned martial arts into a way of life. He is four years older than me. My mother left us when I was three-years-old and I have never seen or heard from her since. This allowed Craig to have the run of the house. And to make it worse, our dad worked afternoons. To politely describe Craig is to say that he was that jerk that nobody liked to see come around while growing up. When we were kids he showed up out of nowhere and spoiled our fun. Most people lose their malice as they get older, but not Craig. Over the years I tried to bury the hatchet between us, but it just didn't work no matter how I hard I tried. Even as an adult he always did things that repulsed me. He laughed when recalling how he drove in Detroit at a high rate of speed with his son Darren after a heavy rain storm to purposely soak black people who were waiting on the side of the road for the bus. He called this game "Puddling." He thought this was such a cool thing to do.

Craig's cohort on our adventures was Chris, my cousin's husband. Once we went canoeing and they just lied on lounge chairs in the canoe and floated down the river, high on LSD. On one occasion they drank nine cases of beer over a three day weekend. The rest of us were wrestling and crashing our canoes into each other, while going down the Pine River and tipping each other over in the frigid water. The river was filled with boulders and trees that were easy to slam into while canoeing. The Pine River is known for its trout fishing and it is one of the fastest rivers in Northern Michigan.

My first exposure to people using cocaine took place during this canoe trip. After dinner Chris, Craig and Lon decided to go into town. As they pulled away in their car they went the wrong way. It was a dead-end street as I found out earlier while running. They came back grinning after the short drive. While talking to Chris I noticed his nose started bleeding and I knew it was from the cocaine. At that moment I knew this wasn't the crowd that I was meant to hang around with because I was going to school to obtain my Master's Degree in Business, I had two kids, I trained regularly and ran thirty miles a week, I worked a full-time job besides doing carpentry work on the side.

When I told my family that I decided to get my Master's Degree in Business, they just laughed. I didn't say I was getting a Bachelor's Degree, I said, "A Masters in Business." I sensed the family having fun at my expense because I was going back to school and they were ridiculing me behind my back, especially, Chris and Craig. I couldn't blame them for laughing because I was pretty uneducated at the time. My dad encouraged me by saying, "The Frenette's are dumb; you'll never make it." Because of that quote I received an all-expense paid trip to Up State New York for a week thanks to the American Management Association (AMA). I entered a contest at Walsh College and wrote a three-page essay paper about what school meant to me. It took me fifteen years to obtain my Master's Degree taking evening classes without ever missing a semester.

Craig joined the National Guard because he needed to make some extra money and he could get out of working at Ford Motor Company. In the seventies, auto companies gave everything to their employees. Craig decided not to go to Camp Grayling and spend two weeks in tents, which was mandatory in the National Guard. Craig said, "Shit, they can't do anything to me. I served my time in the army and they can kiss my ass." He was supposed to report for duty on Friday. Early Saturday morning the police found Craig hiding behind a dresser. They handcuffed him as his two kids watched in horror. Afterwards, they flew him in a helicopter to Camp Grayling located in Northern Michigan. They put him in the brig until he was court martialed.

## Dave

Before I met Dave I used to see him in his yard. Dave looked like a Greek God, with curly jet black hair and he was tanned year round. He was extremely handsome and when entering an establishment, women made google eyes at him and men looked at him because of his size. He was built like the Hulk. Occasionally, Dave went to the Red Doggie Saloon for a beer, but he was by no means a heavy drinker or, for that matter, a drinker at all. The Red Doggie Saloon had a long, shapely glass jug that was filled with coins. It sat on the liquor bar above the beer coolers and in front of the wall-to-wall mirrors that are usually found behind the liquor bottles. Dave was the only person I knew who could lift up the coin-filled jug with one hand with an outstretched arm. Once, he went into the restroom at the Red Doggie and a man followed him in. This guy started ripping Dave's shirt off for no apparent reason; it ended with one blow to the head and his assailant was lying on the floor.

When I was at Dave's house, he asked me to do some cleanup with him on the weekend. I was thirteen-years-old. When we got out of his truck, I started grabbing scraps of wood and putting them in a pile to be burned. Dave laughed and said, "We don't do that type of cleanup; we do carpentry cleanup." I worked year-round doing carpentry with Dave, including summers and weekends. I spent countless hours with him and we appreciated each other. He told me that he got into a fight with a giant, black guy while serving in the army. They fought from the beginning of the train ride until they were almost off the train. Dave said, "I thought I was done for because I was on my back between two seats and lying on the floor while he was jumping up and down on my head with both feet." Dave managed to get up and knocked him through the window of the train and the only thing that stopped him from going out of the train were his knees as he laid hanging backwards out of the train. Afterwards, Dave had to go and see the Army psychologist. The psychologist's diagnosis was that "Dave just liked to fight."

While bird hunting in Michigan with his brother, Sid, Dave was shot at close-range with a twelve-gauge shot gun. The blast picked him up and threw him back five feet and he didn't even fall down; luckily, none of the pellets hit him in the face. Dave mentioned that the blood squirted out of him like it was coming out of a strainer and the doctors never did get all the pellets out because there were just too many of them. Dave complained mostly about the ones in his wrist. If you knew him, you wondered if he had bad karma.

While in the army Dave was a member of the 101st paratroopers. When he jumped out of a plane, the chute wrapped around his legs, and though he managed to get his auxiliary chute to work, it was kind of late. He ended up striking his butt against his canteen while landing. The only injury he sustained was a massive bruise to his buttock. Dave didn't drink often, but when he did, all hell was about to break loose. When he started his carpentry business, he carried a concealed weapon permit. He carried a lot of cash and worked in crime-ridden neighborhoods. Dave loved motorcycles, especially Harley's. Once, while riding his customized Harley through Wixom and wearing his chrome World War II Nazi helmet, he was pulled over by a lone police officer. The cop became belligerent when Dave told him that he had a concealed gun permit. He tried putting the handcuffs on him, but he wasn't having anything to do with it. The cop pulled his gun out, and before you knew it, Dave had taken the gun away from the cop. When police backup arrived to aid the officer, Dave had the cop's gun in his hands, which was an embarrassment for the police department. The incident was dropped and Dave didn't even get a fine.

Once, Uncle Santini and Dave made a deal in which Dave would give him a door-wall and Dave would receive a table saw in return. For some reason, Uncle Santini felt that he had been cheated, so the argument between them grew louder and louder until I heard Dave say, "I think I have just about had enough of this." Immediately, Uncle Santini's demeanor changed and he left without a hassle; it was a wise choice for Uncle Santini. Dave's muscles seemed to expand two-fold when he was angry.

# The Isshinryuist: A Tale of Endurance

It had to be the hottest day ever and we were building a house in Flint, MI. The radio broadcasted one hundred and five degrees. We ran out of water around mid-day and another apprentice went to the store to get us something to drink and the only thing he brought back was beer, and at that time I hated beer and all I could think of was water.  On the way home the heat was making the pavement buckle on the expressway. While we were working in Flint, Dave found some split-frame Harley parts being sold by a woman around eighty-years of age. Dave was trying to get these parts at a bargain and he turned on the charm. She asked, "Would you like some lemonade?" We said, "Yes, please!" It was extremely hot. There was a clothes pole in the yard and I challenged Dave to a contest of chin-ups while she went in for our lemonade.  I was convinced that I would win this contest because Dave weighed a solid two-hundred and forty pounds. They used to call me the worm because I was so skinny, but I always referred to myself as the bear, which made Dave laugh with his infectious laugh. I went first and did eighteen chin-ups. I could smell and taste victory as I savored the moment. It was Dave's turn. He did nineteen chin-ups. I was in disbelief and I felt cheated, but I knew better than to ask for a rematch. The lady returned with our lemonade and Dave turned the charm back on. While we sipped our lemonade, the lady asked Dave to sit on a wooden love seat. It was one of those heavily built log swings coated with four or five thick coats of polyurethane that could hold three people. She also had a full grown boxer that followed her out of the house; this dog liked Dave instantly. As Dave went to sit on the swing, the boxer grabbed a hold of his good leg and pulled it out from under him. Dave's butt hit the swing and he had a dazed look on his face as he sat on ground. It seemed like an eternity went by as I watched him still holding his un-spilled lemonade. But what goes up must come down...the swing went high and when it came down it hit Dave in the back of the head.

One of the Frenette traits is that we tend to laugh when someone gets hurt and we just can't help doing so. I let out a hoot and Dave was on his feet in a second; he forgot all about his charm and the older lady watching us. He was yelling, "I will kill you, you little son of a bitch." I ran around the picnic table while Dave tried to catch me, his muscles and veins bulging. The lady watched us and it didn't seem to bother her at all. At a young age I learned that in order not to get caught I need to run around something. This way the other person doesn't have a chance to gather enough speed to catch me.

Finally, Dave gathered his composure and started conversing with the lady over pricing. He told me that he wouldn't hurt me if I helped him get those parts out of the attic. Dave was a man of his word and his word meant everything to him. It was cramped and hot up there and there was no way Dave could fit in that small space. It was a common occurrence for Dave to be chasing me and yelling, "I will kill you, you little son of a bitch." I didn't always get away either. His favorite punishment was to throw me on the ground, grab one of my wrists and put his foot on my stomach and pull. He wore cowboy boots and I was left completely out of breath.

My parents complained that I was over Dave's house too much, but it didn't stop me. If I didn't go to Dave's house one day, they asked where I was and they told me they missed me. Our family was poor and dad was always quitting his job for one reason or another. At that time most families were poor. Nevertheless, I always had money because I was working every weekend with Dave. I worked with him all summer and we worked seven days a week and twelve hours on Saturday and Sunday. They gave me my official name, "Dickhead." All day long I heard, "Dickhead, I need this or that." Dave boasted that I was the hardest working son-of-a-bitch he had ever seen. We were a team.

Dave usually dressed in jeans, which had to be Levis. He also wore a white-ribbed wife-beater t-shirt and cowboy boots. He had false teeth, but I couldn't tell, or at least I wouldn't have known if he hadn't told me. The reason he ended up wearing dentures was because when he was a kid he whitened his teeth with Comet...He was well groomed and dressed with a western flair and wore a turquoise belt buckle. When he got dressed up it had to be topped with a nice black suede cowboy hat. He was naturally dark as he spent plenty of time in the sun doing carpentry and working on his motorcycles. Dave didn't watch a lot of TV and he had a lot of friends, but they had to come over to his house as he seldom visited anyone. He had three brothers, with him being the oldest. There was Rudy, Sid and Walt being the youngest. Dave had one sister named Holly, which we saw once in a while. The Campbell brothers used to refer to their mother as the "Fucking Cunt." I thought she looked like a toad and was extremely overweight. None of them seemed to like their mother and they grew up fatherless.

Sid was rough and tough like Dave. The other brothers were wannabes. Sid was smaller in stature but had massive arms. Dave told me that he and Sid got locked up for beating up an entire bar in Inkster. It was a topless bar, of course, and after beating up the bouncers, Sid and Dave put their backs together and they just started fighting. He said, "It was amazing that people just got involved and they weren't a part of the fight." His other brother, Rudy, was there and got knocked out early in the fight. For one reason or another they used to always make fun of Rudy, but the Campbell brothers worked together and played together.

I remember going up north with Dave and Sid, and while we were in Standish at Fletchers, a spot for hunters to fill-up with gas, buy food and ammunition, Sid went in a restroom stall but the door didn't lock. Some guy walked in on Sid and said, "Hell, I almost pissed all over you; that would have been funny!" Sid replied, "Until I jumped up and kicked your ass!" The guy quit laughing and took off. There was always something going on while hanging with the Campbell's. On the same trip, after we set up our campsite, these two big burly dudes started yelling that we had better not hunt on their property or they would shoot us. Sid had an ax in his hand because he was chopping on some dead limbs for firewood. He told them, "Why don't you come over here so I can chop your fucking head off!" They left and we never heard from them again. Sid for the most part was a jerk; he wasn't nice like Dave.

# The Isshinryuist: A Tale of Endurance

Dave always drove a newer model pickup and also had a later model car for his wife, Angela. This was different from the way our neighborhood lived. Most families had a stay-at-home mom. Angela wore her blonde hair long and was an attractive, thin woman. They had two children nicknamed Sam and Tater. They were a newer version of the family unit in America. They all liked each other and hung out together. I fit in with Dave's tribe and we were one big, cohesive unit. Dave's friends seemed to enjoy having me being around, too. They liked my quick wit and my ability to lose them as they pursued me around the yard when they grew tired of my humor. I was never exceptionally fast, but I understood how to run around something like a picnic table or a car. Usually, only one gave chase, but sometimes they were all chasing me and leaving me to bolt for home.

Dave decided he was going to build a camper that we could use in northern MI for the upcoming bow-hunt for deer. And, of course, I was involved in this project. We started framing it in with 1"*2" pine. It was pretty cool to have the talent to be able to do something of this magnitude. Every night after Dave came home from work we worked on the camper. It looked nice when we were done, especially from the outside. We went to a trailer store in Waterford and purchased the siding and windows. The camper extended over the cab of the truck that could sleep two people. It had brown paneling on the inside and two windows, a pantry for storing canned goods and a booth for eating. The table folded down for sleeping, plus it had a fridge and a stove. The only thing missing was a bathroom, but we had the great outdoors for that. This was a great time in my life. I was becoming a strong, young man because of the wood I was carrying while doing carpentry. Sometimes I carried for a crew of nine men and they could eat up some lumber. I guess that is why when someone calls me dickhead now, I find it endearing.

It was nearing bow-hunting season and we were excited about going hunting and that we were staying in a camper instead of a tent. There were five of us going hunting: Doug, Ron, Walt, Dave and me; we took two cars. The nice part about deer-hunting was that the weather was exceptional, a change from the often gloomy Michigan skies.

The trip was filled with laughter, stories, jokes and talk about pussy. I knew more about pussy than any kid my age ever did. Everyone was giving me their take on what to do with pussy. How to eat it, lick it, please it and whatever else they could think to do with it. It was like a take out of the movie Forrest Gump, when Bubba talked about all the things he could do or make with shrimp. I always sat in the middle of the truck. Doug rode with us. He was a big guy like Dave but without as many muscles; and sitting in the middle meant that I was going to be punched on from both sides, which would hurt, no doubt.

# The Isshinryuist: A Tale of Endurance

We arrived at our campsite in Northern Michigan. It was on the east side near Lake Huron and about a three-hour trip. We usually went to Luzerne or Tawas. Lake Huron is so large that it looked like an ocean. Ron and Rudy, friends of Dave, set up their tent next to the truck. We got up before dawn and got ready for our morning deer-hunt in total darkness. We snuck into the woods just as it was getting light outside and position ourselves strategically to shoot a deer. Afterwards, we arrived back at the camp to cook breakfast, and given their big appetites, we always had something good to eat. Dave and Doug were getting things prepared for breakfast. I was digging a hole for trash and getting wood for the fire. I was bored with that and went in to ridicule Dave. This was a common occurrence, which usually ended with him hurting me. I climbed into the camper and watched Dave take out a box of wooden matches. When he struck the match there was an explosion that hurt my ears. Dave gave me a big push and I ended up ten feet from the truck on the ground. I watched Doug come crawling out of the trailer on all fours and moving fast. Now, here came Dave. It seemed as though Dave was motionless running on top of the canned goods that the explosion had spewed out on the floor. He eventually made it out with his hair looking like Larry of the Three Stooges. His hair was burnt all the way around. I wanted to laugh, but I couldn't muster a laugh due to the pain. We were all in a lot of pain. Walt was loading us in his car with Dave in the front passenger seat and Doug and I in the back seat. We were all moaning on the way to the hospital. Walt had a Dodge Challenger RT at a time when they made cars fast and gas was cheap. The Tawas hospital was approximately fifteen miles away. I think Walt enjoyed the thought of finding out how fast his car could go. The speedometer reached 180 miles-per-hour. We were going down old US-23 with the speedometer reading 165 miles-per-hour and it still didn't seem like we were going fast enough. Walt's nickname was "Crash" because of the way he used to ride his bike and drive his car.

Upon arrival at the hospital we were piled into three separate beds and were given morphine shots to alleviate the pain. Since Dave was so large, they thought it appropriate to give him a double dose. We all had third degrees burns on our hands; I'm not sure why our faces were not affected. It was almost dark when we got back to the camp and Dave became very ill with chills and started to shake. Ron had been drinking and Walt joined him. Dave and Doug crawled into Walt's tent to lie down. The effects of the morphine made the trees look awesome. A call had been placed to their brother, Sid, to come to get us. When Sid arrived, Rudy and Ron had been drinking for a while and were having a good time. When Sid saw that my bandages were dirty and coming unwrapped he started yelling at Walt and Ron. The reason my bandages were in such bad condition was because I was pulling limbs and gathering firewood to help keep Dave warm while Walt and Ron proceeded to get very drunk.

We left in the morning without the camper and the only thing worth salvaging was the stove, the sink and the furnace. The windows were both blown out and one of them almost hit Ron while he was standing near his tent; it flew directly over his head and he said, "That he didn't even have time to duck." The whole roof was blown up in the air and when it came down, it didn't line up on the camper as it was turned on a 45 degree angle. We pushed the camper off into the woods and drove away.

I remember going to school and not having to write, or do any school work because of the third degree burns on my hands with huge blisters on my knuckles. I still have faint scars on them to this day from forty years ago. This is when I my attitude changed. I started thinking that I didn't need school because I was going to be a carpenter. This attitude was going to haunt me all through my college years. I took as many study halls in high school as I could and I never even finished beginning Algebra. My parents never even noticed what we did in school as long as we didn't bother them.

Dave purchased a small, condemned house on a small located across the street from his home because he wanted to get into horseback riding. The first horse he purchased was a Palomino; it was a gentle horse. It had an easy stride when you rode it. I didn't even have to ask to ride Gypsy. Since, I was taking care of her I could saddle her up and ride anytime I wanted too. This was cool for a thirteen-year-old. There were two rooms to the house and the horse stayed on one side and Dave nailed some 2*4's over the doorway and the feed was stored in the other room. Dave didn't think Gypsy was fast enough for the rodeo-riding we were about to set in motion. If Dave was going to get hurt on his new adventure, it would have to include me, his sidekick, to share in the trickledown effect of pain.

# The Isshinryuist: A Tale of Endurance

Dave bought a young quarter horse he named Randy. He loved this young stud. Randy was beautiful and had chestnut-brown coloring with a jet black mane and tail. He looked like one of the horses in the movies, the lead horse that the other horses follow out of the canyon when the cowboys are trying to capture them. He also had huge muscles on his hind quarters, much larger than gypsy. He was too small to ride because he was still young. He was a mischievous horse that couldn't be trusted, as I later found out, and he was a biter! Every night Dave and I went over to the house and worked with Randy. It always started with us trying to catch him. After a while he ran into the house, where there was no way to escape, which always led to his capture. I left this up to Dave. Not only did he bite, he kicked, too. Dave put a halter and rope on him. He used a small whip to make him go around in a circle while holding onto the rope. Dave was strong enough to handle him if he tried to run. If I had attempted to do this, he would have just dragged me around the yard until he got tired of the game. Later, Dave informed me that it was time to ride him. Randy was getting bigger and stronger daily. Dave told me that he was too big to ride Randy. Dave's weight could cause him to get swayback, whatever that was; I didn't know. This is when he informed me that I was the chosen one and the first one to ride Randy. I didn't want to ride him at all as I was scared of him and he knew it. But there was no way I was going to let Dave know it. It took about a week before Randy got used to the saddle. It was time and Randy knew something was up; I could tell by the way his ears were straight back and how his eyes were fixed on me. He had grown so strong that even Dave was having a hard time controlling him. I looked at Randy and Randy glared at me. His ears suddenly looked like horns. Dave was coaching me the whole time, "Get on him you little chicken shit." Every time I put my foot in the stirrup, he ran sideways almost dragging me to the ground. When I did get on, he was rearing straight up where I thought he was going to fall over backwards on top of me. And as soon as the front feet hit the ground he was kicking with the rear feet. This went on for a long time. Dave held onto the rope and I think this stopped Randy from falling over backwards and landing on me. I was hoping and praying that Dave did not lose his grip on the rope. It wasn't like the movies where the horse walks away and he's broken from there on out. We left the saddle on him for a day and afterwards, I rode him every other day. This scenario went on for a while until Dave let me ride him by myself without him hanging on to the rope.

Randy grew rapidly and Dave was riding him every night. It was time for Dave to start practicing for the rodeo. He brought home three fifty–five-gallon steel drums to practice riding around and placed them like bases on a baseball field. He ran around them and then he raced back to the finish line. Randy was built for short bursts of speed, like barrel-racing. The muscles on that horse matched the rider. Dave was getting good at barrel- racing and he was improving his time. Dave cut the barrel too short one time and his shin got caught on the edge of the barrel. To this day I have never seen such a swollen calf; he even had to cut his jeans in order to be able to wear them. It was always a spectacle when Dave got hurt because he always heard me laughing, while he yelled, "I will kill you, you little son of a bitch."

It was time for Dave's first rodeo; he paid his registration and was riding Randy around to keep him warmed up and to show him off. I was in the stands with Angela watching the other riders' race.

Suddenly, Dave yelled, "Hey buddy, come here." I knew it was going to be something that involved me getting hurt. He told me he just entered us in the pickup race. Randy looked like a monster being fully grown. He was always stepping on my feet and biting me. I was well aware of his antics, and though he never kicked me, he would have liked to, had I given him the opportunity. The idea behind the pick-up race is the rider races at you and then you are swooped up and ride double while racing back to the finish line for the best competitive time. Dave found us a spot where we could practice. Now remember, I was still a little guy who was just thirteen. Dave went down to end of this field and he kicked Randy; they were bolting at me at full speed. It was the Hulk and a monster for a horse. I was scared and I didn't want to play. Dave slowed to make his turn; he grabbed my arm and started speeding back for the finish line. He threw me completely over the horse and I landed on my back in the field. He rode back to see what went wrong. I asked him to stick out his arm and I would swing up myself. Here they came again, Randy snorting and stretching for a full gallop. Again, Dave stretched his arm out, but he didn't help me this time and I was hanging onto the saddle straddling Randy's leg with him running full-speed kicking me in the balls with his thigh. It hurt and I was shaken up and Dave and I were fussing at each other. The loud speaker at the arena announced, "Dave Campbell, you're up." I went down to the end of the field and waited for the whistle to be blown. Randy was all lathered up and ready for action and so was Dave. There was a difference this time; they were coming at me faster. It was a fiasco because again, I couldn't get up, needless to say we were disqualified and I was done with rodeos.

Sid felt left out and wanted in on the action. The horse Sid purchased was a seventeen-year-old Palomino who had been a stud all his life. He seemed to have some Clydesdale in him because he was a mammoth horse. A fool could have picked a better horse. With Sid being Sid, he was going to make his horse do what he wanted him to do. The first thing they were going to teach him was to jump like Randy. This horse didn't even run, if he didn't want to. He just kept walking up to the jump and walking through it and this infuriated Sid.

Barry Sander was there and he knew a lot about horses. Barry had the most beautiful Pinto horse which hosted sky blue eyes. It was an ex-circus horse that could do tricks. Barry grew up in Kentucky and he was extremely scared of snakes. They used to tease him about tying one to his boot. He got so angry when he heard this threat that he told them, "If anyone attempts to do this, I will go straight home to fetch my gun and kill whoever is responsible!" He was really serious about it and Dave knew it.

# The Isshinryuist: A Tale of Endurance

Barry and Sid were going to make this stud listen for the first time in his life. Sid was riding the stud and Barry was taking off his belt. He started hitting the mammoth horse with the belt-buckle as hard and as fast as he could. After about five good hits with the buckle, the horse picked up his rear leg in a lightning quick fashion and kicked Barry in the stomach. He went airborne and was thrown back ten feet and stopped only by a chain-link fence leaving him breathless, dazed and so startled that he could barely get up. Barry never hit that big stud again. Later on, Sid decided to cut off the horse's balls because of its acts of defiance. This was a grueling sight; the veterinarian tied a rope around the soft part of the horse's nose and kept twisting the rope until the horse fell over. Sid lied on the horse's neck to keep him down. The vet tied another rope on his rear hoof and pulled it over the horse's head. The vet went to work cutting off the horse's testicles. The event was over quickly and the stud didn't get up; as a matter of fact, he laid there for days. I thought the horse was going to die. I checked on him daily to see how he was doing; I felt sorry for him. Surprisingly, this didn't change the horse's attitude; he was still a stud with or without balls. Sid finally sold him and he never again joined us for riding, which was fine with me.

Sid didn't have a lot of friends; he was just too damn mean. Once, we went on a fishing trip to Fletcher's Pond. As we were exiting the truck, I said or did something to him that he didn't like. The others were already in the restaurant, including Dave. Sid held me down in the seat and grabbed a steel thermos and started hitting me in the kidney with the thermos to make me apologize. He did this for a long time, but there was no way I was going to apologize. I think he started weighing the outcome of actually hurting me or angering Dave. He went into the restaurant while I walked around outside for a while until my tears dried up. When Dave saw me, he started to transform into the Hulk. I knew he was pissed, but he held it together.

Pressure was starting to build to have Dave move his horses out of the residential neighborhood. A politician even used it as a political platform that if elected he would have the horses removed from Rowe Lake. Soon Dave started looking for a place to board his horses. We went to the Fenton Horse Auction to look at horses on Friday evenings and maybe acquire another horse, but that never happened. The horse auction was crowded and the air was filled with excitement. Everyone was dressed in a western motif and there were horse trailers everywhere.

# The Isshinryuist: A Tale of Endurance

It was at the auction that I found my riding spurs for only three dollars. This is where Dave met Niles and Peggy, who said Dave could board their horses at their farms. The farm was close to the rodeo and just three miles from Dave's house; it sounded like a good deal. I couldn't wait to get back home and try my shiny, new spurs on Randy. I dreamt that Randy would run faster than he ever had. The next day I saddled Randy up and had my silver spurs on my black cowboy boots. This was going to be a glorious day. Have you ever had something planned in your head where nothing could possibly go wrong? Randy didn't have a clue. I didn't think things were going to change, except that Randy was going to run faster, or I would have picked a better spot to mount him: a place without rocks, bushes or vehicles in the vicinity. I mounted Randy and grabbed the reins. I gave Randy a touch with the spurs and he went completely berserk; his nose was almost touching the ground while his rear feet kicked high in the air, then he stood straight up on his rear feet before coming back down. The more he did this, the tighter I clamped my legs around him to keep from being thrown off. Randy was bucking with all his might. I was trying to find a spot where I could let go without landing on a rock or some other object lying around the yard. Dave always had a lot of junk lying around his yard and I didn't want to let Randy choose for me. I ended up airborne and landed on a grassy spot. The only thing hurt was my pride and I never used those spurs again.

I learned early on that horses are the boss when they want to be. We moved the horses over to the farm. There was a large pasture area, a nice barn with stalls and a tack room (a place to store saddles and riding equipment). It was a huge improvement from the house and I didn't have to carry fifteen gallons of water every day five hundred feet away or fill the truck up with hay every other month. This was a win-win situation for me. This boarding wasn't free and Dave had to pay dearly for these luxuries.

This is where I first encountered Maverick. I was prepared for normal horses such as Randy or Gypsy, but Maverick was different. He was the devil in horse form; not only was he big, but he was extremely mean as well and he ruled over the whole farm. As soon as another horse was led through the fence, Maverick galloped straight over to that horse and started biting and kicking it. All the horses shied away from Maverick and only a few people rode him. Somehow they talked me into riding him. I got him in the pasture where the ground was soft. Everyone was lined up against the fence watching me as I rode Maverick. He was doing fine. I rode him through the pasture and down a path that led to another field. I was even starting to have some fun. That is, until we turned around. Maverick put his head down and his ears moved backwards; he started barn-storming. I was concerned for two reasons: First, this was Maverick, and second, the two foot thick cement step that Maverick had to jump on before entering the barn through a small opening. I couldn't pull his head up so I let go of the reins. I used both hands to hang on to the saddle horn as we were heading towards the barn. The spectators formed a line and waved their hands keeping Maverick keeping him from entering the barn. As we approached them I remember yelling, "Go boy, go!" I didn't want everyone to think I was scared when in reality I was having a significant emotional event. Maverick ran around the vast field three times before he settled down and I was finally able to dismount him. Dave's interest in horses waned when he started boarding the horses and had to pay exorbitant fees to have two horses boarded, so he eventually sold them.

Dave was back to what he truly loved, motorcycles, a passion that endured a lifetime. The only motorcycle brand he purchased was a Harley-Davison. He extended the front end and built three-wheelers. He chromed as many parts as he could afford to, or as much overtime as Angela could work. Even though Dave came home every night, they still hired someone to watch the kids and cook dinner. Dave stayed outside in his shed working on motorcycles until darkness fell.

He was proud of the motorcycles that he built. He had one of them chromed everywhere and the front end-extended; however, it was extremely hard to start. It kicked back sometimes and Dave had a hard time from being lifted over the handle bars when it kick-backed. I used to challenge him by telling him I could start that old Harley; and one day he took me up on it. He said, "If you can start it, you can ride it." In reality I didn't believe I could do it. I thought I was going to go over the handle bars if it kicked back. But on my first kick it started. Dave's jaw dropped and he wanted to call the deal off, except that he was a man of his word. He had a lot of money invested in this Harley and nobody rode it but him. I dropped it into first gear and let out the clutch slowly. I never took the bike out of first gear and I kept the clutch in part of the way. I knew I would be dead if I crashed his pride and joy. When I got back to his house he was waiting for me and ready to assist me in getting off his treasured bike. He was afraid I wasn't strong enough to keep it from falling over and he was right...

# The Isshinryuist: A Tale of Endurance

We worked a lot during the summer while I was out of school and we were building homes in Inkster. We built the decks and a semi-truck showed up and positioned itself next to the deck with a crane on top of the cab. I was given a list of numbers and there were numbers tagged to the walls. My job was to hookup the crane cable to the two nylon loops on the walls. This was a stressful job because everyone was yelling at me just to make me nervous while calling me dickhead. I couldn't go fast enough. The walls were nailed together with thirty or forty penny nails, which needed to be pulled before hooking them to the crane. I was always pushing them from side to side to get the correct wall, not to mention that it took all my strength; sometimes the other carpenters had to climb up and help me. Some of these walls were as long as the trailer. The walls were wired, insulated and dry-walled. I knew this wasn't the way to build a quality home. The homes were going to house low-income clients. It seemed everyone else was stealing items off of the house after we left each evening. Items such as: cabinets, carpets and anything that wasn't nailed down. When we came back the next day every window in the house was broken. While we were on the roof, the black kids threw gray alley rocks at us. Besides worrying about falling off of the roof, now we worried about getting hit by rocks as well.

We used generators for power if we couldn't get a neighbor to let us hookup to their power. We had just gotten off break and I went to start the generator, but it was gone! I had never seen such a crime-ridden area. The carpenters even kept shotguns in the corner of the houses that we were building. We were always out of Inkster before nightfall.

Tilley Homes had an armed security guard on site that Dave and I were talking to. He was showing us the extra gun that he carried in his front pocket. He said, "If they try to get the drop on me, they will have to deal with my other pistol." (They found him deceased in one of the basements). Dave was the construction manager, which left me working with Chuck McFadden, who was 100 percent Irish, wiry, strong and with forearms resembling Popeye. He was an okay guy; the other alternative would have been to work with Sid, who would have gladly taken me because of my hard work ethic. The carpenters made me very nervous, so I ran to get everything they asked for and sometimes I took off before they even told me what I was to retrieve.

Dave's brother, Walt, sent me to fetch coffee and doughnuts and gave me twenty dollars to pay for them. After leaving the store and opening the driver's side door of the van, I saw a black dude running across a field approaching me rapidly. I grabbed a bottle to hit him with, if needed. As he came around the front of the truck, I noticed another guy coming from behind the van and pulling a gun out of his pants; he shoved it in my back. They demanded my money. I gave them the cash that was left from the twenty and they didn't hurt me, but after that, I always carried my hammer wherever I went. The funny thing was that I wasn't even scared throughout the ordeal.

Sometimes, on the way home from Inkster, Dave and the crew stopped at a topless bar. I was left in the truck to watch the tools. We parked in the alley because the trailer we were hauling was too long for normal parking spaces. One of their favorite topless bars was La Chambre, off of Telegraph Road in Dearborn. It was an unusual spot for a topless bar. It was in a large strip-mall that also included a restaurant, a drug store and all kinds of little shops surrounding it. It seemed as if we were there for hours, probably because we were. They were all inside having fun and drinking while I was sitting in the truck with the hot sun beating down on me. I was bored and I stepped inside to see Dave, but it was mostly to get a glimpse of the dancing girls. I stood at the entrance to stare at the girls a while longer while they danced on the pole. However, upon entering, I was immediately met by the bouncers. I explained my dilemma, which allowed me to stay in there longer. It became a ritual: I went into the bar and they started coming after me, but just before they could get to me, I made my exit.

On the way home Dave was pretty drunk, so I drove. Dave carried his pistol, which was legal for him to carry. I had both eyes on Dave and wondered, "What is this fool going to do with this gun?" I was never worried about him shooting me unless it happened by accident; but that was exactly what I was worried about, being shot by accident. We were on the John C. Lodge Freeway near Linwood heading out of Detroit. Dave rolled his window down and started emptying his pistol into the embankment. He didn't even look to see if there were any cops around before shooting. Afterwards, Dave had me drop him off at the Red Dog saloon in Milford. He wasn't ready for this fun to end. I drove his truck home and let Angela know that Dave would call her when he was ready to come home.

I found out the next day that Dave had gotten into a fight with Torch. This dude, who was well-built and looked like a Neanderthal, was 6′8″ tall. I remember him well because he threw a piece of ice at me, the kind of ice a snow plow breaks up while scrapping the road. It hit me in the hip-bone and brought tears to my eyes. I was in the seventh grade while he was a senior. I never forgot who he was because he was so tall, and, of course, because of that frozen chunk of ice which almost made me cry. After a couple of punches the fight was over and Dave had slayed another dragon.

Dave, Doug and Ron were discussing Yul Brenner and his latest movie, The Kazaks, and how cool it would be to have their hair shaved like him with one small pig tail coming out the top of their heads using a rubber band to hold it straight up. It was easy to help them get excited about their new look. Before you knew it, the clippers were out and Ron was first; we were all laughing about his full head of hair falling to the ground with each pass of the clippers. When Dave was finished, Ron got up and started feeling his freshly shaved head. Doug jumped into the chair next and was anxiously looking forward to the Kazak look. Dave jumped into the chair next and Doug went to work on Dave's head crisscrossing the clippers and cutting every bit of hair off, but making sure not to cut the pig tail off. They were all proud of their new look. They looked like a bunch of characters out of a Dr. Seuss book. I don't think they would have gone through with this had they not been under the influence of alcohol; they looked ridiculous. At that time I was a junior in high school and hair meant everything. After the laughter died down, they started looking for me. They found me by hearing my laughter from outside the kitchen window. They acted as if I was the one that persuaded them to shave their heads. They were trying to coax me into coming into the house by assuring me that they wouldn't bother me, but I knew better and I left for home.

I didn't go over to Dave's house for a few days hoping their thoughts moved on to something else. I showed up on the weekend but they hadn't forgotten about me. There were a couple of extra people over at Dave's house, besides the Kazaks. When Dave, Doug, and Ron started their pursuit of me, the others joined in and they didn't even know why. I was a lot smaller than the rest of them. I had fear on my side and luckily Sid wasn't there. I couldn't out-run Sid. The other thing I had going for me was that Dave always had junk lying around; there were usually three cars, a boat trailer, motorcycles and a picnic table. I was in my element. I was used to being chased by adults throughout my childhood, along with bullies and my older brother. There were five of them and Ron was a formidable athlete. Once I eluded Ron running around the car and a picnic table, it was time to make my exit by diving over the fence and heading for home. I was fit as a fiddle from carrying lumber, feeding the horses, and doing chores.

Dave and I rode around in his truck going to work, hunting and fishing. We always had a good time laughing and carrying on about how I was going to kick his ass. I told him that, "When I become a black belt, the ass-kicking roles are going to change." He used to get a big laugh out of that. Dave carried his coffee in his green Stanley thermos everywhere and he used to pour it into an empty three-pound can of Maxwell House coffee can. He used an identical one to pee into. Every time he peed in the can, he told me, "If you peek, you have to eat it." I never peeked! I told him that I was going to switch the cans on him; that really used to get him going. He replied, "You better not, you little son of a bitch or I will kick your ass." And to add even more fuel to the fire, I told him that he wouldn't even know it.

When it was time to lift the walls when building homes, everyone gathered on the deck and spread out leaving Dave to lift more than his share. He hollered, "Hey, how about a little help," and then we moved down a little bit towards Dave to help him. When we put up a second wall, someone needed to climb and tie the walls together on top. This task was usually mine because I could climb faster than most of them. Dave dug his hammer into one wall while someone else knocked the brace off from the outside. After this was done, Dave made a ladder out of his thigh and arm. It was the method used to climb the wall most of the time, but if I wanted to add some excitement to this, I used the top of Dave's head for my third step. He'd have a fit; he jumped in the air trying to punch me and I moved back and forth to get out of his way. I knew it would involve pain for me later, at a time when I couldn't get away.

My favorite thing to rile Dave up was when we were putting up the trusses, I took the middle of the trusses because you only need one nail and the journeyman carpenters were much better at nailing. I taunted Dave until he couldn't take it anymore. He caught me when I couldn't let go of the trusses and he walked to the top of the walls until he was in front of me with my stomach exposed. He threw about four or five punches at my stomach knowing I couldn't let go of the trusses. He didn't try to knock the wind out me, but I could feel the punches. Then I waited for him to get back to his spot. Afterwards, I yelled to the crew, "Did you see that? I took everything he had and I'm still standing." The crew and I started heckling Dave. He pretended he was getting mad, but everyone was having fun. None of the crew was exempt from being teased.

Dave, the crew and I went to Northern Michigan for the weekend to build a house. Dave put on a new pair of Levis jeans. There seemed to be some type of a curse against him whenever he put on a new pair of Levis. I saw this happen to him three or four times while we were together. Dave started talking to the owner about his dirt bike. And before we knew it, both of them were racing their engines at the starting line. Ron was using his hand as the flag and when his hand dropped, they were off. Dave was on his Sportster and the other contestant rode a 350 cc Honda made for dirt-riding. Dave's bike spun a lot of dirt in the air while taking off. The Honda took the lead as they sped away, but we could see Dave gaining on him. We lost them when they rode through the woods, and when they reappeared, the Honda was ahead by a couple of lengths with Dave closing the gap. Dave had a big grin on his face as he was approaching the finish line. Just as Dave passed the dirt bike, he hit a large bump in the make-shift road and his bike went airborne. Dave went about eight feet high and flew a distance of about fifteen feet. The bike went one way while Dave went the other. When Dave came down, he landed on his head and I saw his neck fold under the weight of his body. When Dave got up on his feet, his first few steps were wobbly. I knew he was hurt, but he didn't want anyone else to know it. He displayed an extended grin as a cover up. We ran over to see if he was okay and to congratulate him on his win, though it really was a loss in my book. The Harley was still drivable after the crash, but Dave confided in me later that he had a headache for nearly a week after the accident.

Pinhead

The first time I noticed Tony was in Junior High. Three people were chasing him and he was really small. As students were headed to their next class, he kept diving through their legs escaping the clutches of the people that he had just pissed off. The next time I saw him he was in my study hall. He called this kid a dog-killer because he was accused of killing dogs in Lake Sherwood, which was the most affluent neighborhood in the area. When the teacher left the classroom, the accused was larger than Tony and two years older than him, jumped on Tony and knocked him to the floor. Tony was trying to protect himself from the kicks that he was receiving. Dog-Killer was giving it to him with both feet in rapid succession. I was thinking, "I should try to break this up." But I kept hearing this dog-like yelp coming from Tony every time he was kicked. I knew he was a cool guy when he acted like a dog being beaten and that's when our friendship flourished. He was a smart-ass and he was damn good at it. When Tony caused some type of disturbance in class, the teacher immediately called on him for an answer hoping to embarrass him, but he always knew the answer. One of his greatest attributes was that he was like the Football Hall of Famer, Gail Sayers he could hit full-speed in three steps.

My friends, Tony, Bill and Chris would jump up and down when they saw me driving down the driveway. They knew we were going to have a good time because I was going to buy some refreshments and afterwards drive around the back roads drinking and getting high. We particularly liked listening to the Cheech and Chong cassettes.

We went to a party in Walled Lake which was located down some winding cow pasture roads. I don't even know how we found it or who told us about it. We were in Tony's car, a small, black Buick with a metal dash. Tony's alias was Pin-Head. He was fun to hang around with and he was absolutely brilliant. Most of the kids at this party weren't happy to see us because we were from a rival town and hitting on their women being macho nineteen year olds. We had a round tin of powdered snuff. This snuff could really clean out the nasal passages. I was using Pin-Head's nose to challenge others; no matter how much they snorted, I gave Pin-Head more. At the last challenge we were all laughing. Pin-Head's challenger had just snorted a fair amount. I dumped as much snuff that could hang onto my folded index finger for Pin-Head to snort. Bill laughed while telling me, "Don't! You will kill him!" By now Pin-Head had the attention of the whole party. I stretched my arm towards Pin-Head's nose and, yes, he was up for the challenge. Everybody was laughing and waiting. Tony gave the best snort of his life. After that magnificent snort, he fell down on the road while everyone laughed.

At that point, a car was leaving the party and it was driving through the crowd and heading towards Pin-Head's skull which was positioned directly in the path of one of its tires. Unfortunately, none of us could quit laughing long enough to tell the driver to stop. I was holding my crotch to keep from peeing because I was laughing so hard. Finally, another friend, Jordan, got his act together and yelled, "STOP" as loud as possible. We pulled Pin-Head out from under the bumper of the car and decided to leave. We piled into Pin-Head's car and drove away.

As we left the party and started heading down the twisted roads, we saw two teenagers waving us down and wanting a ride. "There isn't any room," Pin-Head told them. "But you can ride on the trunk." Both of them climbed on the trunk and Pin-Head started driving fast and this made the two hitchhikers start swearing and beating on the window, but mostly searching for a hand or a foot-hold. Pin-Head thought that because they yelling that they were having a good time. I glanced at the speedometer and noticed we were traveling at 45 miles per hour. It was a dark night with a full moon and we were staring directly into their frantic faces through the rear window. They were still yelling and shouting obscenities. The Buick weaved around the road making it feel as if we were on a roller-coaster ride. When we got to the gravel road, Pin-Head stopped and rolled down his window to talk with them and to see if they liked the ride. I could see their faces illuminated by the brake lights. When they jumped off the car, they started hurling rocks. I extended my foot across the hump and stepped on the gas while Pinhead tried to have a conversation with these two guys. The tires spewed gravel all over our assailants as we sped away.

Moments after reaching the pavement, a car pulled up next to us and someone threw a beer bottle against our window, but it bounced off. The car was full of teenagers from Walled Lake, our nemesis, including the two guys that were riding on the trunk. Chris started crying, but I assured them, from previous experience, that they couldn't break the window with a beer bottle. The Buick couldn't lose them because they were in a fast muscle car, and every chance they got, they pulled up next to us trying to break our windows with their bottles. Pin-Head held his cool and pulled up in front of the Milford Pool Hall for help. Everyone got out of the car and started fighting; I remember getting punched in the head because I quit fighting when the police pulled up. The people that were inside the pool hall poured into the street for action. The police quieted down the mini-riot and sent us home.

My friends and I decided to go camping for the weekend on my Dad's property in Gladwin, Michigan. My dad owned ten acres and I had never been there before. We could buy alcohol at age eighteen because of the Vietnam War. The voters decided that if we could die for our country at eighteen, we should at least be able to buy beer. We were headed for a three day trip over Memorial Day. It was funny that this trip on Memorial Day weekend turned out to be so "memorable." The same people from the snuff-sniffing contest were with me, plus one more and I drove. I had a pretty nice looking car, that was, before the trip. It was a red Chevy Impala in mint condition. When we arrived, our first dilemma was the weeds, which were so high we couldn't see anything. I thought we were going down a road until the side of my car struck a huge boulder. I couldn't go forward or backward without scratching my car. Finally, I just had to drive off the boulder leaving a crease down the entire passenger side of my car. Everyone had a good laugh over it, except me.

The next thing we did was head into town and stay for last call at the bar. We weren't done having a good time yet, so we decided to play hide-and-seek in the weeds when we got back to the property. The weeds were chest-high and swayed back and forth due to heavy winds. We couldn't find Pin-Head (Tony) so we gave up and he won. Then Pin-Head yelled from the top of a tree. This tree didn't have limbs close to the ground making it extremely difficult to climb. And if this wasn't enough to discourage someone from climbing it, it took two or three of us to reach around it; it was a massive White Oak. Nobody could see Pin-head, even with the big flashlight. I retrieved my shot gun from my car and I was just going to shoot the leaves on the edge of the tree. Bill saw me gathering my gun and I thought he was going to stop me, but he was encouraging me instead. Pin-Head yelled, but we couldn't see him anywhere. We were circling the tree using the flashlight. I loaded the gun; we all laughed. Pin-Head didn't have a clue about what was going on.

After the gun shattered the silence and pellets sprayed the leaves, Pin-Head yelled, "I'm coming down; don't shoot." With the help of a flashlight, we saw him rapidly coming down. We were laughing hysterically; then he fell. He was up 40 feet when he fell. When Pin-Head hit the first branch, he looked like a giant squirrel with arms and feet outstretched. Bill was doing a good job shining the flash light on him. We could see him spin in different directions as he hit the branches. We could even see the expression on his face as he hit the ground with a solid thud. He landed with his head bent between his shoulders. He groaned loudly and only had the wind knocked out of him. I would have preferred to fight Benson (my sensei) than fallen from that height. Most people don't survive a fall over fourteen feet. Charlie yelled, "Pin-Head's dead!" We all laughed, high from the weed and the beer. Again, it was Jordan who ran over to see if Pin-Head was alright. He was still breathing, but he was in shock. Immediately, I started thinking of an alibi because I believed Charlie was right and that Pin-Head was dead or soon-to-be. After all, how could anyone survive a fall from such a height? Pin-Head didn't want to go to the hospital though I pleaded with him to let us take him there. I thought without a doubt that he must be bleeding internally. I was afraid we'd find him dead the next morning. I woke up early and checked on him. He said he was ok. I told him that I wanted to buy him breakfast, but he said he just wanted to sleep, so I left him there with Bill and headed for town.

# The Isshinryuist: A Tale of Endurance

We drove into the town of Gladwin, which is located in the middle of the state and is known for its hunting and fishing and little else. Chris and Jordan joined me for breakfast. Mark Twain once noted, "All small towns are alike." He hated small towns. At the table, our conversation focused solely on Pin-Head's fall. We agreed that he must have fallen between 40 to 50 feet. In spite of this accident, we thought it had been a great night.

We had gone into the restaurant looking for the big man's breakfast. It was a typical northern breakfast where a few locals hung out to drink coffee, read the paper and talked about the weather. After ordering our breakfast, I headed for the restroom since there were no facilities on the land. I was hoping to be back in time to eat my breakfast as it was laid down on the table, steam oozing from it. But when I came back to the table, I saw two men who were dressed like cowboys, sporting cowboy boots, cowboy hats and wearing turquoise belt-buckles that looked like they could stop a bullet. They also had a deep southern drawl. I sat down and introduced myself, Chris excused himself because he felt he was going to be sick, probably because he had too much to drink the night before. A few moments later Jordan left and headed for the car. Now I was getting irritated because I had to pay for their meals and they didn't even touch a thing. So I ate my meal as I talked to the Texans. They were two wiry guys without an ounce of fat on them and probably around thirty-five-years of age and short in stature. They could have probably qualified to fight in the 135 pound category. We must have talked for over a half hour, which made me think we were going to end up being friends. As far as Jordan and Chris were concerned, they could sit in the car until the cows came home making me waste my hard earned money. So I said good bye to the Texans and we shook hands.

Now remember, this is 1972 and we are pretending to be hippies. Chris and Eddie looked like hippies. They wore their hair long and their jeans were frayed from walking on them. They looked like they smoked dope. Chris wore a head-band to show he was of Indian ancestry. I also had long hair but didn't fit the hippy status quo because I always dressed nicely. I bought all my clothes at head shops because I made a lot of cash doing carpentry.

Chris and Jordan started to tell me about the two Texans. The Texans were telling them that it had been a long time since they had kicked any hippie's ass because there weren't many hippie's in Texas. They said, "We are going to kick your asses and make it look like a saloon fight." Afterwards, they were going to jump in their rigs and drive back to Texas. The action was about to begin, that is, until I came out of the bathroom and sat at the table. Chris and Jordan said they sure were glad that I came out of the bathroom when I did. When they saw that I was fit as a fiddle, it made them change their minds. They didn't say anything to me about fighting or I would have obliged them. At the time I was a Roko-Ku (orange belt) and working on getting my green belt.

As we pulled down the road headed towards the property, it was great to see Pin-Head walking around. He said his ribs were really sore from hitting the branches on the way down. He thought he would be able to get a hold of a branch on the way down and said, "He was never worried until he hit the ground."

It was time for another adventure and we decided to go down to the State Fair in Detroit. Bill was our other crew member. The three of us hung out together all the time, a troika. Bill had just bought a new Chrysler Duster. He was a year older than Pin-Head and he and was working as a brick laborer. Pin-Head and I were finishing up our senior year. We were off for a Friday night adventure and carried our usual bag of weed. We always had a great time, or at least two of us did. Bill was proud of his new car. We pulled into a crowded State Fair and Bill took extra care parking his new car. As soon as we went into the State Fair, we lost Bill. We never laid eyes on him again until the State Fair closed. We went back to the car several times to see if Bill was there, but we never found him. We left without him to enjoy the shows and rides. Pin-Head and I were having a great time, along with making some of the carnival people mad at us. We went back to Bill's car a second time; I checked the door to see if it was unlocked. The button had some slack to it, so I pushed it in some more and something snapped. Pin-Head was on the other side of the car and didn't believe me so he pushed the other button and he broke the other door button. Wow, we knew Bill was going to be pissed, but we decided to go and have some fun and worry about the door buttons, later. The Jackson Five were playing at the fair before they became popular, so we decided to watch them and maybe find Bill in the process. We went to the car a third time when everything was closing. Bill was next to the car when we arrived. We asked him if he had a good time. He was upset over not being able to find us and said, "No, I didn't have a good time because all I did was look for you the entire night." It was time to deliver the news to Bill about his car. We told him about the buttons and he seemed to get more upset when he couldn't get into his new car. To make matters worse bill opened the trunk to get the tire iron and we had to pry open the vent window, which broke in the process.

Still looking for trouble, we decided to drive down Woodward Avenue and wound up in Pontiac. We saw a hooker and decided to ask her some questions about prices and other things. We were all laughing until she saw the tire iron on the floor. Then she motioned to a car behind us. The lights from the car started shining through our windows while this gal was freaking out. We were telling Bill to take off because there were four big, black dudes in the other car and it looked like they wanted to do us bodily harm. They were in pursuit and trying to get us to pull over and we couldn't lose them either. I tried to calm Bill down by telling him that they couldn't get us out of the car unless we stopped. We thought they were going to shoot us through the windows. I recognized where we were and guided Bill to the police station parking lot, and, luckily, they just drove off.

On our way home we stopped at the Weal Bar to have some beer and shoot some pool. We laid our quarters on the pool table to reserve our spot. We got busy drinking, laughing and telling Bill he shouldn't have bought a Chrysler. When I looked at the pool table I saw only one quarter. I went up to the pool table and put the only quarter in my pocket. This meant that Bill would have to argue with someone for his quarter. Bill and another guy started trading insults back and forth. This led to all of us being kicked out. The argument carried out into the parking lot and they started fighting. Pin-Head and I coached Bill through the whole fight. The guy gave up when Bill repeatedly slugged him in the kidneys.

# The Isshinryuist: A Tale of Endurance

During my senior year in high school I worked at Glen Oaks Country Club in Farmington after school and weekends. I worked as many as sixty hours while going to school. My Dad hired me while he was the chef and this is where I met Fred Polski. Fred was in college. He could open his throat and drink a sixteen-ounce beer in under three seconds flat. We made money by asking Fred to challenge other people to down a glass of beer. Sometimes they quit drinking just to watch him perform this feat of magic. After he finished a can of beer, he smashed it against his forehead. He did this in front of the ladies to impress them, but that didn't work.

Fred's driving was far from typical; it was more like riding with a race-car driver. From Lansing, Michigan, he could make it to Orlando, FL in eighteen hours. Fred said he drove at speeds of a hundred and fifteen miles an hour to get there for spring break." When he came back from Florida after spring break he had a cast on his arm. It took me a week of asking what happened before he told on himself. He said that he was driving down I-75 with his friends partying and speeding through a construction zone at night. He told everyone in the car to watch the blinking light on that barrel because, "I am going to knock it off with my arm." He struck the blinking light with his arm. They immediately got off at the next exit to look for a hospital. He didn't know the barrel was filled with sand and that the blinking light was securely bolted to the 55 gallon drum.

# The Isshinryuist: A Tale of Endurance

While Fred's parents were on vacation we had a party at his house. Fred was a big guy who usually hovered above the rest of the crowd. He knew I was taking Isshinryu and we started sparing in his basement. We punched and kicked while all our friends watched. When Fred moved in for the kill, I took his feet out from under him and he landed on his forehead. The carpet ripped several layers of skin off his forehead and the confrontation was over. Fred seemed embarrassed that I was able to do that to him. He thought I got lucky. His forehead was oozing a clear liquid and everyone was teasing him saying that his head was going to be sticking to the pillow when he woke up.

On another occasion, Fred didn't take defeat easily and was ready for another try as we left the bar. We squared off and started sparring in the parking lot. He attacked and got in close; I ended up kicking him in the elbow with my shoes on. This made him let out a yelp as he backed away and decided the fun was over. Afterwards, Fred was a believer in Isshinryu and never sparred with me again. He later told me that he was excited because he was so close to me that I wouldn't be able to kick. Isshinryu is designed for close in fighting. In Fred's latter years, the same elbow swelled up on him like a football and he had to go to the hospital to have it drained. He blamed it on that thirty-year-old kick.

Fred mentioned that we could visit him anytime. It was Friday and Fred's first year at MSU and he was required to live on-campus. We arrived at the campus dorms around 10:00 A.M. We called Fred from the phone booth a few feet from his room. I asked if we could visit him today and he agreed. We knocked on his door thirty seconds later. He was still in bed and crabby because we showed up almost immediately.

# The Isshinryuist: A Tale of Endurance

At a dorm party everyone was discussing politics or theories, something we weren't used too. We all liked the way women looked and dressed in college. We started downing the brews until someone brought out some hash and told us how good it was. Well, come to find out, Pin-head and Hash didn't mix; it was like giving an Indian alcohol. After he smoked the hash, he went into a comatose state and lied on the bottom bunk-bed without moving. His eyes were open, but he wouldn't say a thing. Bill and I just kept drinking. We knew Pin-Head was a survivor and could handle anything. Other people became concerned and sent someone to get the Resident Assistant (RA) to take a look at him. He concluded that he was okay, but told us to keep an eye on him. Bill and I went out into the hallway to visit others. When I came back to the room, there was no sign of Pin-Head. I needed to use the bathroom, but I couldn't get through the door and it was unlocked. I had Fred help me push the door. We kept ramming the door to move the obstruction…until I was able to see what was stopping the door from opening and I realized it was Pin-Head's head. I thought we had knocked him out. He was trying to tell us that he had to use the bathroom. I held him up, but that was as far as I was going to help him. He started peeing, and when he was done, his glasses fell off and he didn't have enough coordination to pick them out of the toilet. I worked his elbows like a robot to help him fish his glasses out and he succeeded. I got him back to bed and went to find Bill again. When we came back to the room, we realized Pin-Head had disappeared again and it was late. We went looking for him, first inside and then outside of the building. There was a blizzard outside and it was a large campus. Bill and I decided to go back inside and find a couch to sleep on. We decided to look for Pin-Head again later. We later found him sleeping inside his car though it was fifty degrees below zero including the wind chill factor. We all headed back to the dorms to finish sleeping.

Pin-head and I smoked some Moroccan hash while working at the Country Club. I was able to get him upstairs to the bedroom. I laid him on the bed. His eyes were wide open and they never blinked and remained open for hours. The workload was light and I could handle it. I checked on him regularly as his eyes stared aimlessly at the ceiling. I decided to have some fun with him and told him, "Pinhead, I called your dad and he's on his way." But his eyelids never moved, though I could see just a little glisten of a change in them. I knew he understood me, but he never moved. I went downstairs to continue working and to cover for him, as he would have done for me. He later came down and told me I pulled a good prank on him. My adventures with Pin-Head were coming to an end because life was pulling us in different directions. As a matter of fact, we never had a disagreement. If you never had a friend like Pin-Head, you missed out. We complemented each other in spite of having such different backgrounds and coming from different ends of the social spectrum.

### Early Training Days

When I was seventeen, I got the mumps and I have never been that sick. I was helping my friend shovel horse manure when I realized I was becoming sick. The experts advised never lift anything heavy while having the mumps. A few days later, I was delirious and I could've care less about anything. I was out of commission for so long that Dave came over to visit me, which was extremely rare. He laughed so hard when he saw how big my head was, but I could care less and I went back to bed. Then it happened…the swelling dropped down to my balls. It was like someone had cut the sack open and sewed two grapefruits in there. I was afraid my nut sack was going to explode! I am flat on the bed with my legs wide apart to give them more room to grow. When the swelling went down I was left with little ball on the right side. The only difference was that when little ball got scared, it didn't come back down right away and it caused excruciating pain. Balls are extremely sensitive to begin with, but, with little ball, you could add twenty times the sensitivity to it. I became a great orator in front of the doctors that were getting ready to examine it. Some doctors told me they would not touch little ball. That said, I could feel little ball smile again.

There were two things that made me proud when I turned eighteen. Uncle Santini used to shake our hand and squeeze it. He was strong and he wiggled his arm back and forth, which kept him winning longer than his years should have let him. He grabbed a hold of my hand and squeezed, he shook my arm vigorously, but to no avail my concentration was on the squeeze. After a few minutes he finally said, "That's enough Lar." That was the last time he ever stuck his hand out to squeeze mine.

# The Isshinryuist: A Tale of Endurance

The other time was when Craig came home from the Army after a tour in Vietnam. Remember, he was the only reason I started studying martial arts. My day of reckoning was here! Craig said, "I heard you have been taking karate." Everybody has had their ass whipped at one time or another, and if they say they haven't, they're usually lying. Craig had been kicking my ass since deliverance day and I respected him as an opponent. I was concerned, but nothing was going to steal this moment from me. Mark Twain stated in his book, "Life on the Mississippi, "That nothing good comes from being a coward." I wasn't sure what devious strikes Craig may have been taught while in the Army. I only knew what Benson had taught me about Isshinryu. Dave taught me that if I punched someone in the head, they would never mess with me again, whether I won or lost. And I wasn't above resorting to this if I had to because the days of Craig beating on me were over forever.

Craig asked me to fight and we went in the basement and we set the ground rules that I learned from Sensei Benson about sparring. He agreed, but I never trusted him. I knew he would resort to any tactic to win. We went into a guard position and started striking each other. He charged and moved back after I delivered a few kicks to his mid-section. I was smiling and happy knowing his reign of terror was over. He punched me a few times, but not the way I hit him. He realized that whoever was teaching me Isshinryu knew what he was doing. Afterwards, he didn't say I word, but I knew I got the best of him. Later, he also started studying Isshinryu under Sensei Benson.

# The Isshinryuist: A Tale of Endurance

I was fit as a fiddle when my kids were small and I was making up my own triathlons. I ran in all kinds of weather, from one hundred and four degrees to minus fifty with wind chill. I ran in thunderstorms, hail, ice and high winds. I made it to the point where I could run six miles in thirty-six minutes even if hills were involved. I only made this time on a few occasions. The first time I ran ten miles I discovered I had muscles that held up my shoulders, before that I never gave it any thought. I also discovered that I couldn't out-run horseflies and that a t-shirt rubbing up and down on my nipples produced scabs. To remedy this I bought myself a giant jar of Vaseline and rubbed it on my nipples. As for the horseflies, I stuck a t-shirt over my head and flipped it back over my shoulders; this gave me an Egyptian-like appearance, but it worked.

I never used ear phones to listen to music. This would have violated one of the principles of Isshinryu: "The ear must listen in all directions." I have battled many dogs and never lost a confrontation with a dog since studying Isshinryu. I credit this to my dedication to train. I was nearing the end of a run and I was dog-tired. A black, mid-size dog came off the porch. There was a young child watching his dog go after me. Dog's nails make a different sound on cement when they really want a piece of you. When he got close, he leaped in the air going for the tender spot above my knee. I had been bitten there before by a Jack Russell and it had been one of the worst bites that I ever received. I could feel his teeth sinking in my leg. The next thing I knew, the dog yelped and knocked back on his haunches and the child started crying. I always say, "Weak feet will let you get beat." The kick I used on the dog was a Mae Geri (front kick) which I refer to as my bread and butter kick.

# The Isshinryuist: A Tale of Endurance

I never lock myself into a technique; it just happens. The Lady/Serpent on the Isshinryu Patch is (Mitzi Gami). If you pay close attention to the Isshinryu Patch, Mizti Gami has one hand raised in peace and the bottom half is a serpent in turbulent waters. This is how a karate-ka is supposed to carry his or herself, at peace with everyone, until provoked. Dogs are territorial, so when you notice them, the key to getting away is to run and to put as much distance between them and their property.

The reason that I am still able to run is that I avoid hard surfaces. I have seen a lot of runners retire before their time because they didn't heed my advice. They don't run a horse on concrete, do they? I ran beside the roads or pavement paths found in parks. This is why I am injury free to this day.

I was married at the ripe age of nineteen. It was about the closest thing to a shotgun wedding that you can come to. My bride to be was Tammy Pilson. I had violated Gene's Pilson's daughter and he wanted marriage. I was in love with Tammy and was proud to marry her at the time. The proceeds from the wedding netted three-hundred dollars, which was just enough for a down payment on a trailer that was ten feet wide and fifty four feet long. I was officially tagged as trailer trash, but I didn't mind. I had a journeyman's card with the AFL-CIO Carpenters Union and I was getting paid a Journeyman's wage.

The trailer manager referred to me as 34, my lot number. He didn't like me much either. We were going through one of those contractions in the economy. This caused me to pay my rent late. There wasn't work to be found anywhere. I was applying at 8:00 a.m. at any place that would hire. Many places had signs posting "No Openings." Finally, Tony got me a job painting planes for cash. I was paid $3.50 an hour, which was very discouraging, but at least I was working.

Dave arrived home from Arizona after working there for over a year, but here was something amiss when Dave came back. He always wanted me to help him with stuff and I had my own life plus I was married. I was training regularly and I was starting to run like Forest Gump; running came easy to me. Dave was building a new house and thought I should be over there all the time working for free. I had a family on the way. I guess Dave looked at me as though I was still a boy. Dave was the foreman. We had a guy on the crew named Martin Odell. He was thin, muscular and about six feet four inches tall. He had red hair and freckles. This all came with a bona fide temper. He was nicknamed the orangutan because his calloused knuckles seemed to drag the ground and we teased him about it.

I was setting windows with Martin and we were inside a roughed out bathroom where there wasn't much room to begin with. Martin had a wonder bar (small flat crowbar) and was trying to move the window. The crowbar got stuck in the window. Martin was feverishly trying to remove it, first with one hand and then with two hands. Finally, the Irish temper took over and he lifted one of his orangutan-like arms over his head and smashed it with his open hand. The bar moved a quarter of an inch. Martin was furious and wrapped the injured hand under his arm pit. Then he started kicking the bar with both feet. I hid behind a wall until the tantrum was over. At least he was smart enough not to hit the bar with his other good hand.

# The Isshinryuist: A Tale of Endurance

At lunch, Martin was talking about how he used to beat a bag that was attached to the ceiling and to the floor. He said that he worked out with it for many years and was proficient at hitting it. Somebody suggested that we should fight. Martin accepted immediately and there was no way that I was going to back down in front of Dave and the crew. I told him that I would bring in the foam hand-pads soon and we could go in a vacant home and spar. I thought Martin was going to kill me with his temper alone; I'm only an orange belt. I brought the foam gloves in on a Friday. A homeowner brought some cases of beer for us because they were always excited to see their new home being built. The other guys stayed to drink beer and Martin and I headed to a vacant house. I was nervous because I was thinking Martin was going to kick my ass. My true sensei talked about never getting nervous before the altercation and that you have all the time in the world to be nervous afterwards. The only problem with this is that he wasn't my sensei yet. I gave Martin his gloves and he put them on immediately. The foam pads weighed about two ounces. It was full contact to the head. Martin was excited. We touched gloves and let the festivities begin. Martin was swinging hard, and every time he swung, I made him miss with a side-to-side movement. I was busting his nose every time he swung and the kicks were taking a toll on him. I beat the hell out of him and his face was reddened from the punches he took. Martin called it quits after he figured out that I was punishing him badly.

When Martin and I came back in the house, Dave and the crew were still drinking. Martin told them that I whipped his ass and that there was nothing he could do about it. I will never forget the look on Dave's face because he couldn't believe it either. Martin had taken my place with Dave and I left the crew shortly after. It was easy to find a job back then. I used to joke that if the foreman threw a hammer at you and you caught it by the handle, you were hired.

My wife was giving me grief about being gone so much, and to appease her, I started training at home more and less at the dojo. I thought I was getting good, but I didn't have a clue how bad I was as a martial artist. I wasn't really learning anything at the dojo. I had a basement, a bag and a chunk of carpet. Most of my students were relatives, friends or friends of the relatives, and, to top it off, they were paying me. I would stretch them out and we did a grueling workout and fight. I would have kicked their asses like Benson did mine, but I didn't have his skill. I can't reiterate enough on how not to be a sensei. At that point I didn't need to be teaching martial arts. I had on average about seven or eight people to train and to spar with on a weekly basis. I was in hog-heaven thinking that people thought that I was good enough to teach them and they paid me fifteen dollars a month. I followed the exact format as Benson, which was, "Let's just kick their asses," Craig would even come and help me beat on these poor souls. Mr. Sutton was an orange belt from Benson's Dojo. He came over to fight in the basement and we had an agreement that he wouldn't let Sensei Benson or anyone else know. Mr. Sutton knew how serious this was because he had a taste of Benson's knuckles. One night, Craig was fighting Mr. Sutton and put such a beating on him that I had to stop it. Mr. Sutton was game because, if he got beaten, he was right back for more. Now, don't think that I didn't like Sensei Benson; in reality, I idolized him.

# The Isshinryuist: A Tale of Endurance

I trained my cousin Waylon and he thanked me because of an incident that happened in his life. It was raining and the wipers were struggling to keep the rain off of the windshield. He was working in Ohio and installing heating and cooling units in large factories. While driving home and near the Toledo/Michigan exchange, he almost missed his turn and moved over quickly causing an accident. Two cars pulled over to exchange information. When the drivers approached each other, one driver punched the other driver in the head, though he had nothing to do with causing the accident. Waylon was able to see the confrontation because the street light was directly above them. He was a couple hundred yards in front of them. The one who was punched was holding his jaw and ran over to Waylon's vehicle to get away from the irate person. Waylon told the guy that he was going down there to talk to him. The other guy told Waylon, "I wouldn't do that if I were you. He is really pissed." Waylon surveyed the situation before walking towards the two vehicles. The irate driver was running around his car kicking it. And then he looked toward Waylon and yelled, "You!" The irate driver took off of his jacket and threw it on the ground. He charged like a mad bull towards Waylon. Waylon told me he was nervous and all he could think about was the Mai Konate kick (heel thrust) that he learned while training with me. Waylon delivered the heel-thrust kick and it landed just below the solar plexus and it took him right off his feet. Waylon jumped on top of him and hit him a few more times, until the other guy didn't want to fight anymore.

I closed the basement dojo, not because I wanted to, but because warm weather was upon us and the people I was training had better things to do. I was a chump beating on people who had zero skills. I headed back to Benson's dojo. Summertime always held opportunity for me in training. The karate-ka's that were close to me in rank and that had been getting the better of me in kumite were surprised to spar with me in the fall after they took the entire summer off while I trained.

At this point in my life I had to keep extremely fit because I never knew when an unannounced Shodan might show up at the dojo wanting to kumite. I was the one they threw in first to see how tough he was and it allowed the other Shodan's a chance to find a flaw in his fighting style.

# The Isshinryuist: A Tale of Endurance

Benson

I worked hard in and out of the dojo. I finished all my fifteen upper body exercises along with my lower body exercises, which consisted of eight kicks. We had grueling workouts led by Sensei Benson's Shodan's (black belts). The classes were an hour and a half in length, which included stretching, punching, kicking, situational awareness and kumite (fighting), which we did a lot of. If you did win in kumite, you weren't always a winner because the injury you received while fighting your opponent meant that you had an injury that would last for months while the other karateka usually walked away with only the wind knocked out of him. I always said, "All good injuries last a year."

I learned my first two katas: Seisan and Sanchin. A kata in its simplest terms is an encyclopedia of moves; it is nothing but "pure" movement. You don't change the movements in kata because they need to be passed down to future generations of Isshinryu students the way Tatsuto Shimabuku (Founder) passed katas down to his students as taught on Okinawa. Isshinryu is derived from two styles: Gojo Ryu and Shorin Ryu. Gojo Ryu is the father and Shorin Ryu is the mother and Isshinryu is the child. Shimabuku changed the principles of the art, which meant he needed to change the name. Being an Isshinryu practitioner means that you can slide over to Shorin Ryu or the Gojo Ryu side depending on what you are doing for bunkai (application).

# The Isshinryuist: A Tale of Endurance

Gojo Ryu is a hard style with hard strikes and blocks. Shorin Ryu is a soft style consisting of blends and fooling your opponents' mind while delivering powerful strikes. Isshinryu has several katas, from both Shorin Ryu and Gojo Ryu. The only original kata to Isshinryu is Su Nu Su. This kata was made up by Tatsuto Shimabuku. It is considered to be the most difficult kata by many because of the balance needed while doing it.

I was up for promotion and I went to a Hockey Arena to purchase a groin protector. It was big and I wanted it. The cup would protect the pelvic bone and, hopefully, my balls. I showed up at the dojo (practice area) after work and I was hoping that Sensei Benson wasn't going to be there. He greeted me as I entered the door. He said, "Frenette, don't forget to wear your cup and bring your mouth guard, too."

It was my first promotion, but it wasn't a class promotion, it was just Benson and I, which meant that I got beat up by Benson with only a few people watching. I was worried all week when Sensei Benson told me to prepare for orange belt (Roko Ku). Nothing works correctly when you are doing your katas in front of your sensei. It doesn't matter how well you are prepared. You will fall apart when you bow in to start the kata. I made it through Seisan Kata on my first try. It was Sanchin, the breathing kata that gave me trouble. I was on my third attempt to do Sanchin correctly when Benson was interrupted by someone who entered the dojo and was asking for directions.

# The Isshinryuist: A Tale of Endurance

I was sweating thinking that I was going to get beat up without a new belt and lose my thirty dollars for the cost of the promotion. And wouldn't you know it...a black belt was standing behind Benson. He was showing me what I was doing wrong with my hands. His name was Sensei Babins. I did the kata for Benson again and he was pleased enough to tell me to go and put on my fighting gear. I ran to the back room like I wanted to fight him. As soon as I got behind the door, I hung my head low. I wanted to yell like Nancy Kerrigan, "Why me?" When I reappeared, I was all smiles, but it was a facade. Benson faced me and I faced him. We were both turned sideways to protect our extremities.

He didn't even have a mouth guard; my heart sunk. I didn't think he would beat me up too bad because I was a newbie. The thought on Benson's mind was to kill while mine was to survive and stay as close to the mirrors as possible. Benson loved his mirrors and he stopped fighting long enough to pull me away from the mirrors. Wow, was I wrong, at first he played with me and then he threw a kick so hard, it took both forearms to stop it and it hurt. His demeanor changed every time he kicked; it was to demonstrate his power. He didn't have to convince me because I saw him beat up everyone. He jumped in the air and was going to deliver a shuto (over hand strike) to my head. I went to block my head and he delivered a Yoko Geri (side kick) to my ribs. The fight was over. I couldn't continue or breathe either. He didn't waste any time in beating me to a pulp. Benson was picking me up from behind and chuckling while putting some air into me. Benson had me line up in front of him and we did a formal bow. He told me he was pleased to have me as a student and that I worked hard. He gave me my orange belt and I turned around to put it on, which showed respect. You never tie your belt in front of someone, especially in front of a sensei. After I tied the belt, we did a final bow and I went home on cloud nine.

Afterwards, I was just scared to fight him, but I wasn't afraid to fight other people. There is a saying in Isshinryu: "Many people will come through these doors, but few will remain." I can attest to this. I have met hundreds throughout my Isshinryu career. The way Benson broke my ribs the first time didn't teach me a thing about fighting and it hindered my ability to become a good karateka for years to follow. A karate student should be brought along like a fine race horse. There will be a time when you are going to give him some punishment, but it will be determined later to see if he is going to stay. When I went back to do the dojo, I was sporting my new belt and I was being congratulated by the other ranks. I showed up on a Saturday and there were just a few people around. It wasn't a formal class; you just worked on what you knew, but there was someone there who could teach you something. Benson made sure the floor was covered with a brown or black belt for instruction.

# The Isshinryuist: A Tale of Endurance

The only people at the dojo this particular Saturday were Benson, another black belt and a brown belt. I bowed as I entered, (which is like saying hi to everyone) and I went over to the mirrors to work on my basics. A few moments later, the brown belt walked over to me and asked, "Would you like to Kumite?" I noticed Benson watching. I responded, "Yes." and I went back in to the changing area and put on my goalie cup and my mouth guard. This was my first Kumite with my new rank. Benson liked to officiate and watch the Kumite matches. I heard Benson yell, "Ijame" and we started trying to land blows on each other. The brown belt was pretty good and he was getting frustrated that he couldn't put me away because of my conditioning and my reverse (the ability to move backwards quickly), which put me out of harm's way. Benson was coaching the brown belt because he was the higher rank between us and should win. All of sudden, he threw a Chinto pivot to extend the reach of his rear punch. I wouldn't have a chance to be out of his range, but that wasn't my intention. I threw a mule-kick that landed on his abdomen while he was outstretched; it took the wind right out of him. He was done for and he couldn't continue to fight. I heard Benson let out a big laugh and yell, "Point Frenette." I bruised the ego of the brown belt in front of his Sensei. I knew that I would need to keep my eye on this guy because I knew he would be looking for revenge.

Again, I went home feeling proud. I'm not a super star or anything like that; I just got lucky. I don't feel I have a natural ability for the martial arts or even an athletic ability. I just try to outwork everyone. I train and I train hard. I was getting beat quite often and my body was covered with bruises.

I have never told this to anyone, but Craig wanted to steal a couple of Isshinryu patches from the back room at Benson's Dojo. I was supposed to be on the lookout. I wasn't really into it because of the consequences, but I agreed to it and I am as guilty as him. I was supposed to watch the door while Craig stole the patches. Now I know how the guy who drives the getaway car during a bank robbery feels. Craig came out and said, "I grabbed two, one for me and one for you." I pretended I had to go to bathroom, but my real motive was to make sure Craig didn't put them in my bag. I kept the patch and left some money on the counter a few weeks later to pay for my patch.

Benson explained the eight kicks taught in Isshinryu and how they could be executed inside a bathroom stall with the door shut. It's amazing how many people have misunderstood this concept and given me the desired win when they closed the distance thinking that my hands would be my only weapons. Remember, people sporting those giant arms can only walk on their arms for less than fifty feet. I continued working out at the dojo on a regular basis and even had bruises on my back.
Sensei Rufus was a strong, conventional fighter that demanded respect from everyone. When you first start fighting you take every blow head-on instead of using a deflection. Rufus' only intent was to make you a good Isshinryuist. He wouldn't beat you up like Sensei Benson. I felt there wasn't any reason for this behavior; any sensei can do that to a beginner. While sparring he'd stop the session and tell you what you were doing wrong, but if you didn't correct it afterwards, he nailed you and you never made that mistake again. Sensei Rufus was different when he fought other Shodan's in the dojo. He put most, or all of them, away except Benson.

# The Isshinryuist: A Tale of Endurance

When Sensei Cotton went up for his black belt, he fought Sensei Rufus and Rufus punished him. At the end of the match he slugged Cotton in the jaw. Cotton left for Arizona after his promotion and when he came back to the dojo, he told me that he had to drink from a straw for a month after his encounter with Sensei Rufus. Everyone in the dojo liked and respected Sensei Rufus. He led most of our warrior workouts and he was going to make gladiators out of us. The first time I met him, he told me that he had just gotten out of the hospital after getting in an altercation with five people. He said, "I took three or four people out and I would have won if I had used eye techniques." He was a solidly-built guy that you wouldn't mess with for fun.

Our karate school entered a tournament. There was a tall, black belt that was faster than most and that knocked out two of Benson's black belts during sparring. One of them was Sensei Smith, who I thought could possibly beat Sensei Rufus because he trained so hard. This was when Sensei Rufus wasn't showing up at the dojo regularly because of his business interests. I thought Benson was going to spar, but Sensei Rufus volunteered instead. The fight was scored on points and Sensei Rufus was losing badly. He was frustrated because after the guy struck him, he took off. It was the last point that the other black belt needed to secure the win. This time Rufus charged and he couldn't get away because the judges' chairs were in the way and he was falling over them. Rufus hit him with a full, bare knuckle-punch with his ribs outstretched. The other guy won, but he really lost. Benson encouraged us to do tournament-fighting against other martial arts styles and different Isshinryu schools too.

# The Isshinryuist: A Tale of Endurance

Sensei Rufus was training us in a sparring session. The guy he was sparring with was using a Seichen stance (Iron Horse Stance) incorrectly and had his ass sticking out. He warned him once then Sensei Rufus kicked him in the ass so hard the dude screamed. He never stuck his ass out again and I learned from his mistake as well. It looked like it hurt. The way you learn techniques in the dojo is when someone hurts you with one of their techniques. You think about how much it hurt and you then practice the technique over and over again until it's ingrained into your fighting style. Benson emphasized, "It's better to argue from a court room than from a wheelchair. "

Craig had great respect for Benson. We were working out in the dojo while Benson was in his office. He came into the dojo and told everyone to put their fighting gear on. There were usually around fifteen people that meandered into the changing room. You could hear a pin drop because nobody talked. We all knew what was about to happen. He told us to lineup and sit comfortably. Benson started at one end of the dojo and beat us up according to rank and you knew exactly when your turn was coming up because he never went out of order. It became more realistic when the person next to you got up. After my beating I could watch with anticipation and hardly anyone ever laid a blow on Benson. He was like a fox in the hen house and, with ease, had his way with us.

Benson had an arsenal of weapons to throw against us. When he moved, you reacted. I was concerned with his hands and his feet. When he kicked, I used both arms to block. He specialized at doing what he called a "forty five." He'd stood in front of you and made a movement and the next second he was beside you punching and kicking. When you tried to get away he tangled up your feet with his and then he fell on top of you. It ended with Benson applying some type of arm bar in an attempt to snap your elbow. You felt helpless and you wanted it to stop instantly. One of the cool things about fighting Benson was the drive home and how proud you were to be alive. After fighting Benson, not many people scared me. When Benson moved into his new dojo, he fixed it up nicely. He didn't charge me much in dues because I was doing carpentry for him at the dojo. This new dojo didn't have a weight room, but it had an area for one. Instead, Benson made this his personal training room. We had to sign up for a half hour of private instruction, which involved fighting and kata. He charged each of us thirty dollars and it was mandatory. Benson made sure this sheet was signed by everyone in the dojo and it increased his cash flow considerably.

Sensei Griffon, a black belt at the school would punch us in the chest bone for no apparent reason. It happened when we were talking to him and it was uninitiated. When he started walking around everyone shuffled away from him and nobody wanted to talk to him. He was mean, strong and trained relentlessly. It was like watching a mean dog walk around the dojo. The new students caught on quickly. I knew Benson wouldn't approve of this behavior, but I wasn't going to tell him. I just kept my distance because Sensei Griffon lifted a lot of weights and took steroids. He eventually died from drug use at a young age.

There were a lot of black belts that came to the dojo and most of them were nice and helpful, unless Benson was instructing them while they were sparring with you. Rick Thomas was one of his students and a good one. He trained hard and he did cardio training on top of it. We feared fighting Sensei Thomas. Once while fighting Sensei Thomas, I popped him in the jaw and he yelled. I thought I was done for, but instead, he exclaimed, "Good technique."

Sensei Benson started full contact fighting, which meant we wore protective foam padding on our hands and feet. This meant you could kick and punch the head as hard as you wanted and it was up to the other person to defend themselves. This was when I started to see the world light up. While growing up, the cameras took one picture on one flash. It was so bright you couldn't see anything after the picture was taken. When you get hit in the head real hard, you see a flash and the world lights up.

Craig told me that he fought Sensei Fowler a few days earlier and said, "He was hitting my head like a paddle with a rubber ball attached to it." Sensei Fowler was smacking him at will and there was nothing he could do about it. Craig was scared of Sensei Fowler and so was I. He was new to our dojo and was a high-ranking black belt when he started. He used to fight as a professional boxer in Canada, even Benson had a hard time fighting Sensei Fowler.

One of my proudest moments was when I went down to the dojo on a Saturday. As I reached the door, I started summarizing who was at the dojo that could destroy my morale. Fowler was walking around with sixteen ounce boxing gloves ready to spar. I jumped past the doorway where he couldn't see me and to check if there were any other high-ranking dons around. I was a first degree brown belt and the highest ranking belt there. There was nobody there to stop Fowler from beating on me. Being the man that I am I jumped across the doorway again and I went home without being seen by anyone. I didn't even feel bad about being a chicken. After listening to Craig talk about the beating he took from Sensei Fowler, I didn't want any part of it.

Benson was having a full contact match in Pontiac, and guess who was on the roster to be one of the undercards? Craig and I went to watch because we wanted see Benson fight full contact and we were sure that he was going to win easily. The fight was to be held at Pontiac Northern High School on Friday evening at 7:00 P.M. Our dojo was fighting against a Korean school that trained out of the Salvation Army, also located in Pontiac.

# The Isshinryuist: A Tale of Endurance

It was Benson's turn to fight. Everybody was excited and we thought that he was going to have an easy win over the other sensei. Benson struggled in the full contact arena and he struggled with the other sensei. Benson fought in the middle class weight of 165 pounds. Benson did win the fight, but got punched often and his opponent wasn't backing away. When the fight was over something happened and Benson was going after someone. Three people were restraining him, and while this was happening, another big guy snuck up behind Benson and punched him in the head. Benson turned around and then the wildest thing happened. The three people who were hanging on to him went flying as if they were on a carnival ride.

Benson started going after the guy who hit him, who, in turn, was going in reverse as fast he could. A bunch of people jumped between them and the arguing started between all the members of the club and the people in the stands. It was close to becoming a mini-riot because the other dojo was black and ours was mostly white. I 'm not sure what stopped it, but finally everyone calmed down and went home peacefully.

I took a private lesson with Benson when he was practicing his full-contact fighting. I was seeing the room light up as he kicked the hell out of me as if it were a professional match. I was used to Benson quitting when he got me down, but this time it was different. It was one of those beatings where you have to break away and you're proud of doing so. Benson was sitting on my back and I was on all fours. I was giving him a backward horseback ride and he was slugging my kidneys repeatedly. I was running so fast on all fours that he fell off. I was hurt and I was starting to dislike him. When I got home, blood was in my urine and I was sore for a hell of a long time.

# The Isshinryuist: A Tale of Endurance

My respect for Benson was waning because of the beatings I was taking and he wasn't really teaching me anything because he didn't know how to translate katas into bunkai, nor did he care to. I was starting to lose sight of why I had gotten into martial arts, and that was to defend myself, and not let some of the things that happened to me as a kid continue, in my adult life.

The first time I had heard of bunkai (the application of kata) was from a black belt named Sensei Barrett. He came from the west coast and trained in a couple of Isshinryu schools that were taught directly from Shimabuku. He talked about extending one's thought and energy. I wasn't aware of this type of training and my cup was full where I couldn't take on any new ideas because we didn't train this way. I liked training with Sensei Barrett who taught for Benson on Saturday mornings by himself. He taught us new exercises and we didn't always spar. We learned techniques from kata.

I was up for my second brown belt promotion with Benson. I wanted the promotion, but I knew a terrific beating was involved, along with me passing my kata instruction. There were lower ranks and five brown belts going up for promotion. We paid thirty dollars for our promotions. On promotion night, the school was filled with spectators. After the chairs were taken, there was standing room only. Bones was a brown belt that taught at the school for Benson and was going up for his third brown belt (san ku). Bones was a good guy but nothing special as a fighter. We would spar with no outright winner.

For our promotion we did our katas first. And every one of the brown belts didn't pass their katas on the first try. I remember doing all of my katas a couple of times before being able to get through them. Poor Bones couldn't remember his katas and wasn't going to get promoted, but he enjoyed a free fist festival. At least I was going to get a higher belt over the ordeal. Benson was humiliated in front of the crowd and it was because his brown belts weren't able to do their katas. It was bad enough fighting Benson when he was jovial. This was going to be different. It was the perfect storm: there was a crowd and pretty women. Benson loved to show off in front of a crowd, and, especially, in front of gorgeous women.

Benson ordered us to put our fighting gear on. At those words, the crowd became excited and restless. We hustled into the changing room because nobody wanted to enter the dojo last. The silver-lining was that I forgot about my bills. Benson was a sixth don and was wearing his candy striper belt for the promotion. The belt consisted of multi-colored patches of red and white in equal lengths of five inches. When we bowed in after dressing, we made a straight line with shoulders touching the person next to us. Benson told us to sit comfortably. We had our shin pads, foam footies and foam gloves on, along with our cups and were holding on to our mouth guards.

Bones looked scared, and to add salt to the wound, Benson walked by him and threw a used tissue on the floor and told him, "Hang on to this; you're going to need it." The color left Bone's face and I couldn't help telling Bones, "I'm glad I'm not you." He looked like he wanted to cry. Even with the funny line I had just laid on him, he wasn't any happier. I had my own concerns.

# The Isshinryuist: A Tale of Endurance

I was fighting a spider in human form. My strategy was to use mirrors and let him call me back out on the spot to fight. He usually grabbed me by the GI and pulled me to the center of the room. Hey, this was serious business. I could get knocked out or he could be riding my back in front of the crowd. My other strategy was to stay away from his hook-kick. He could lift that front leg up and kick you on the far side of your smile line and snap your head with his heel before you could move. I saw him knock a lot of people out with that technique.

Bones was called up to fight, but I wasn't really worried about him because I was thinking about my own hide. I got a flash-back of a previous promotion. Again, the dojo was packed and I was out there fighting Benson. I was running away. He grabbed me with both hands around the back of my head and kneed me in the groin. I was in the air parallel with the floor and hovering about as high as Benson's head. I landed in that exact position on the floor and I never moved. My ears were working perfectly and I could hear about thirty people clapping. I couldn't breathe either. The wind was knocked out me and Benson was laughing. He was picking me up trying to get some air into me. At this moment, I think Benson was the happiest.

# The Isshinryuist: A Tale of Endurance

I am two people away from Bones and getting ready to spar. This was psychological warfare and it worked. Benson asked Bones, "Do you want the head gear?" Before Bones could say anything, Benson continued, "You will need it." Bones latched on to the headgear like it was something treasured; he stuffed his mouth guard in and slipped the headgear on. It was a foam head gear and made out of the same foam our footies and hand pads were. The pads were bright red and glossy. When you used the head gear, it left a blind spot for a kick to come straight up and rattle your head. Benson could bend like Gumby. Benson and Bones faced Sensei Thomas who was judging the confrontation. Benson and Bones faced each other and bowed and assumed a fighting stance. Bones was going through the formalities, but his heart wasn't in it. Thomas yelled, "Ijame" (begin) and Benson was setting Bones up for the kill. He was slugging and kicking Bones repeatedly and from what I saw, Bones needed two helmets instead of one. The only people having fun were Benson, Thomas and the spectators. The psychological warfare was going through the ranks as we all watched in horror; even more so for those that had ever enjoyed a beating by Benson.

My last hope was that he would let some of us fight Thomas and that I was going to be one of them. Bones bowed out and looked like a beaten and despondent man, especially because he would receive another beating for his Shodan belt, so this beating was free! The next man in line was called up and I used to whomp all over him. He was an insurance salesman who wore thick glasses. Benson asked him if he wanted the head gear and he declined because he needed his glasses. Benson was light on him because he didn't have the head gear on and gave him an average beating. The next student wore the head gear and received a terrific beating and got caught with Benson's hook kick and went down for the count.

# The Isshinryuist: A Tale of Endurance

I was next, and though I am no mathematician, I figured out that wearing that head gear wasn't the way to go. When I fought Benson I used the mirror strategy, but I got caught with the hook kick in the left shoulder and fell over backwards. Benson was on me instantly. He used an arm bar, which ended the sparring and I was home free. Now I could enjoy the rest of the promotion. We were given our belts and I was now a San Dan, Nikyu (second brown). You don't change belts; just your rank and you line up closer to the front of the line.

Benson was going through a divorce and was closing down the dojo and we were looking for somewhere to train, it was as though someone had dropped a bunch of BBs. Some of the practitioners switched styles, others quit and Benson went to Florida and dropped out of the Isshinryu scene altogether. It was the end of an era. After Benson closed the school in Pontiac, I started training with Sensei Tom Seth. He was about five foot-nine and had a full head of black hair and was exceptionally strong. It looked as though he lifted a lot of weights. I studied there for about a month and when I was stretching out my body I stared at Sensei Seth and I was amazed at the size of his head. He must've been intelligent because studies show that the larger the head is, the smarter the person.

Sensei Seth was having us do Sanchin kata (breathing kata) and he was going around performing different strength tests on us. When he was in front of me, he slugged me in the pelvic bone. I dropped to the floor because I didn't have a cup on. His students were required to wear a cup at all times. This was different than at Benson's school where we always had time to put on our fighting gear. From then on, I wore my cup at all times.

Pilson's

The Pilson's, my in-laws, were a unique bunch known as "the outlaws." I liked Gene the best though it wasn't always that way. When Tammy introduced me to her family, what unfolded seemed to come right out of a reality TV show. Gene worked at Ford; he was very religious and belonged to the John Birch Society (Radical group of the sixty's-seventy's era). I managed to ruin his mood for a couple of days just by taking an opposing view.

Her mother's nickname was Tweets. She sported short, gray hair amidst streaks of black. She had false teeth, which she pulled out frequently and her regular apparel consisted of a nightgown. She was extremely overweight and permeated the air with her body odor. The odor was so pungent that it engulfed me as soon as I opened the door. Tweet's arms were larger than my head. Her diet consisted of coffee, cigarettes and bologna sandwiches with Mayo. She was a fixture of the couch. When I used the upper story bathroom I noticed some brown gunk in the wastebasket. It took me years to figure out that this substance was powder snuff, which added yet another vice to Tweet's bad habits. On one occasion she displayed her entire breast in front of me, so when I dealt with her I always wondered was ulterior motive and it how it was going to haunt me, later. I believed the only reason God put her on this earth was to make my life miserable.

Wait, there were more Pilson's to add to my misery. There was Gil, Torrey, Jorge and Monica. Jorge was eleven-years-old and so fat that he couldn't sit in an adult lawn chair. Gil was involved with the mafia. Torrey didn't work, except in spurts to procure something frivolous like a horse. He switched churches frequently after the congregation gathered enough money to get him and his wife, Monica, out of financial trouble. Torrey was father to five children, but only one looked like him (one of his kids looked Chinese). Torrey and his wife had black hair, yet their children's hair was as diverse as the colors of the rainbow. It seemed that everyone had sex with Monica, except me. She was cute, pencil-thin and had long hair that reached below her waistline. Torrey's 12-year-old nephew, Gabriel, spent the summer with Torrey and Monica. Gabriel and Monica would ride the dirt bike into the woods to have sex. When Gabriel left at summer's end, Monica appeared sad. Gabriel was happy to return the following year. It took Torrey two years to figure out they were having an affair. Torrey had two Mormons excommunicated from the church because both of them had sex with Monica. When Torrey secured a steady job at Ford, he and his wife moved to a mobile home park where he lived next to his best friend, Tom. Torrey caught Monica and Tom having sex the day before Thanksgiving. In spite of this, Monica, along with her family, showed up for Thanksgiving dinner at Tweets' house. That evening Tweets and Monica got into a brawl at the front door. They started ripping at each other's clothes with Tweets winning; her excessive weight helped her succeed. Though I was not present, someone later compared it to a fight between a Jack Russell and a St Bernard.

Tammy, my wife and I attended a wedding in Algonac, Michigan. I sat at a long table along with Tweets and her family. Tweets drank alcohol and quickly started feeling its effects. While seated with Tweets' family, she asked, "Larry, you don't like me, do you?" "Wow. What a loaded question," I thought and quickly responded, "No," while I stared at everyone at the table. The matter went no further.

At the wedding, the alcohol loosened Tweets' tongue. She told one of her cousins that she owned a 650 BSA that was just sitting in her barn and that he could have it. In fact, the motorcycle didn't even belong to Tweets; it belonged to Gil, her stepson. Tweets' cousin's eyes lit up at the thought of snagging a free motorcycle and he later crossed four states to pick it up. Tweets had to retract her statement when he arrived at her doorstep. She told him that the motorcycle wasn't hers and that he couldn't have it. The cousin then drove back to Virginia without even saying goodbye.

At the Pilson family gatherings my goal was to arrive early and leave first. The less time I spent with them, the better. I took pleasure in asking everyone to move their car so I could leave. Everyone then had to back out onto a busy street with a 50 mile-an-hour speed limit.

I took up running and I always carried my running shoes with me when we went to the Pilson's. I ran nine miles to go home, which only enhanced my Isshinryu training. I was in school at this time, so when I didn't want to go to the Pilson's, I came up with the best excuse, "I need to study. There is a test coming up."

# The Isshinryuist: A Tale of Endurance

I was still practicing the flying kicks I learned at the Korean school. I would have quit doing them had Benson embraced the eight principles of Isshinryu. He never mentioned the principles in spite of having them listed in his professionally-made pamphlet. I only became aware of their existence after reading the pamphlet.

The Isshinryu principle, "The body must be able to change direction at any time" is the reason you don't see jump-kicks in Isshinryu and it's also the reason you don't see Isshinryu on television because it isn't one of those glamorous head-kicking styles. Shimabuku didn't intend for his style to be turned into a competition. Yes, Isshinryu does have head-kicks, but usually your opponent is on his knees or is bent over.

Tammy, my cousin and I were walking downhill through the dirt trailer park roads. They were ahead of me when I decide to do a flying-kick at the back of Tammy's head. She wasn't very tall, which enabled me to reach that height. I started running towards her from behind and with a leap I got into the perfect form to deliver a flying-Korean-kick. I had one leg tucked underneath me and the other foot was extended (the way the Koreans do on their ads for TV and newspaper). It felt good, though I could not hold this pose for long or risk hitting her head violently. I decided to curl up in a ball to avoid hitting her. I was unable to stop and landed on her shoulders. She fell and slid face-down she was livid. I was surprised she didn't get hurt.

## Sensei Roald

I discovered that Shane Roald, one of Benson's black belts, was teaching at the CAI without a contract and charged less than Sensei Seth. I enjoyed training with Sensei Roald. Mr. Roald's school offered two evening workouts compared to Benson's school, which was open six days a week. The first night there I met my future sensei, ("Sensei Cotton"). He was wearing dress clothes and sporting long hair. He sat on the sidelines staring intently at me with his crazed, gray-blue eyes while I trained. He was probably wondering who I was and strategizing how to bury his knuckles deep into my flesh. This was the start of what I will later refer to as, "His reign of terror." I noticed he was in great condition, but I didn't know that he was a karate-ka until two days later when he showed up wearing a black belt. In Roald's dojo we used the old style and Kumite (bare-knuckles) and bare feet, but we still wore a shin-guard. The worst thing that could happen here, besides having Benson show up, was to kick someone's elbow, even with a shin pad. This meant that you created a bruise on the top of your foot that will hurt every step of the way while wearing shoes. I could tell that Sensei Cotton couldn't wait to fight me.

The first night at the dojo some individuals started tinkering with his car. Sensei yelled out the window, "Get away from my car before I come down and kick all of your asses." I knew he meant it, too. Sensei Cotton had been trained by Sensei Roald. When I started training with Sensei Roald he was a fourth don. He fondly recalled the first time he was introduced to Isshinryu. He was at the CAI building and target-practicing with a bow and arrows. He noticed people going into the bathroom and coming out wearing white pajamas while carrying their shoes and clothes up the stairs and disappearing behind a door.

# The Isshinryuist: A Tale of Endurance

Sensei Roald followed them one night up the stairs and was allowed to watch the class workout. He was instantly hooked and went back the following week. Two marines came into the dojo and wanted to fight. Sensei Benson informed them that it must wait until class was over. Benson made everyone leave, except Roald. Sensei Benson asked the marines, "Do you want us to put our shoes on or do you want to take your shoes off? The marines were disappointed in their own hand-to-hand combat skills. They became a fixture on the floor. After this, Sensei Roald started training consistently with Sensei Benson. Sensei Roald said that Benson was doing a demonstration for the Detroit Lions and strongly explained how, "I woke up on Alex Karras' (football hall of fame) table with Alex clapping vigorously and roaring with laughter." Another time, Sensei Benson hit Roald in the face and shattered his cheek bone. The surgeons repaired it through a crow's-foot-wrinkle located below his eye. After this incident, Roald was done with exhibitions (join the crowd...).

I was never concerned about fighting Sensei Roald, but I was concerned about fighting Sensei Cotton, who brought to mind the song, "A Boy Named Sue" by Johnny Cash...He kicked like a mule and bit like a crocodile." I knew firsthand that Cotton was the top-dog in the dojo. We fought often and it seemed as though I was fighting for survival. One evening, after fighting each other, he came over and said, "Frenette, look what you did to my knuckles!" His knuckles look bruised and swollen. I rolled up my Gi sleeve to show him where he hit me. My elbow was turning dark blue and swollen twice its normal size. Cotton seemed proud to have inflicted such pain on me and strutted away. My arm felt useless and I wanted to let it hang like a broken chicken wing, but never in front of an opponent. I considered this psychological warfare. My advantage was to have him believe that I was really tough. At least this is what I hoped he was thinking.

# The Isshinryuist: A Tale of Endurance

I was a second degree brown belt (Ni Ku) and had been a brown belt for more than a decade. Promotions have never been a priority to me. Sensei Roald informed me that I was up for promotion. My friend Chris McDonald was with me and Sensei Roald let him know that he was up for promotion, too. I recruited my carpenter friend Earl to come to the dojo and he was going for his orange belt. Chris didn't handle pressure well, which made me feel better, but I was nervous. Words could not express my feelings at knowing that I did not have to fight Benson. Sensei Cotton will get some good kicks in, but it won't be the kind of beating that Benson would inflict. At this stage of my Isshinryu career, I was terrified of Benson. We had a week to prepare for our upcoming promotions. Everyone liked to come to the dojo to watch promotions. Roald was a businessman and charged thirty-five dollars for the belt and promotion. I worked on my katas every night after work. Earl and Chris only had two katas. I practiced seven empty-hand katas for speed and power. In addition, I had two Bo katas (weapons) to demonstrate as well. I washed and pressed my GI. I was ready to go and I didn't let Tammy attend the promotions because I didn't need her telling everyone how I got beat up. When Tammy found a weakness, she sure could exploit it.

On the way to the dojo my side mirror collided with another truck's mirror. I knew it was my fault because I was preoccupied. I arrived at the dojo and surveyed the situation. I saw my future sensei, but no Benson. This was my first promotion without him. I checked twice making sure my goalie cup and mouth-guard were in my bag. Earl and Chris were in the restroom and almost dressed. They were not interested in talking.

# The Isshinryuist: A Tale of Endurance

Roald instructed us to line up according to rank. My friend, Fred, was standing next to me. He would secure his Sho Dan (black belt). Sensei Thomas entered the dojo and we didn't invite him. Even, Sensei Cotton was no match for him. It wasn't my lucky day. Sensei Thomas displayed his fighting gear on the outside of his bag. The shin-guards looked worn out. Sensei Thomas was about 6'2" and in amazing shape. He was a weight-lifter with a cardio regime. His student followed him into the dojo. Ricky was a shodan and we trained at Benson's school together. He was about 5'9" and had long, black hair, which he tied into a pony-tail. He trained exclusively with Sensei Thomas. I categorized him as a light-weight. After we finished katas, we sat down. The lower-belts fought first while we watched. Sensei Roald and Cotton took turns fighting the lower-ranks. It was Chris's turn to fight Sensei Cotton. The match was one-sided. He didn't beat Chris to a pulp like Benson would have, but he gave him a good shot to the kidney.

It was time for Fred to fight Ricky. Ricky nailed Fred with a kick to the solar plexus and it was over. I saw the look of disgust on Roald's face. It was my turn to fight. Sensei Cotton was doing the ceremonies and my first opponent was Sensei Roald. We both turned towards Sensei Cotton and the three of us bowed. Sensei Roald turned towards me and we assumed a fighting stance. Cotton yelled "Ijame" (begin). We moved back and forth...Sensei Roald's signature technique was deflecting strikes with the ability to reach the far kidney with a shuto (open-hand strike). He nailed me with a couple of these and we bowed out.

Afterwards, we went through the same ceremony again, but Cotton was now my opponent. I fended off all of his attacks and held my own. After we bowed out, I noticed that he shook his arm in disgust implying he didn't nail me like he wanted to. I knew Sensei Thomas was next, but Ricky lined up instead. He thought he was going to beat me like he did Fred at the sound of "Ijame." Ricky started delivering lightning-fast kicks, which I eluded. He launched another attack and I responded with an ouchi (wide punch) nailing him on the sternum with my bare knuckles, which caused him to blurt out a yell. In our next exchange his finger got smacked and was broken. The "kumite" (fight) was over. The ku's were summoned in front of the four shodans (with Sensei Roald hosting the ceremonies) and we formally received our belts. Everyone was given a different color, except for brown belts. The same brown belt is worn for the three different rankings in Isshinryu. Everyone got their promotion, which isn't always the case. I was not sure why Sensei Thomas didn't join in the kumite. If he had, the outcome would have been different because he was tough; I was happy he didn't. I trained with Thomas for many years and admired him as a sensei. The highlight of this event, besides it turning out to be my night, was that my friend, Chris, received his orange belt and I was proud of him. It was his only rank, but it meant so much to him. Chris let out a victorious yell and headed home clinging to his "roko ku" orange belt. After the ceremony, Mr. Roald confided in me, "Larry, I sure was proud of you tonight." Earl and I met our wives at a bar. We were ready to celebrate.

# The Isshinryuist: A Tale of Endurance

There was always something exciting happening at the dojo. We were allowed to spar with anyone to improve our fighting skills. When the time to spar neared, we all sat down according to rank. We never knew who we'd be matched up against; rank didn't matter and it was left up Sensei Roald to choose. There was one student that Sensei Roald talked to after he was through fighting. It pertained to his habit of sticking his tongue between his teeth while fighting. He later sparred with Roald's son. I was working out in front of a mirror, when I suddenly saw people heading towards him and sensei's son. I noticed there was blood all over the floor. It appeared that he stuck his tongue between his teeth was bleeding heavily from his mouth because Roald's son had kicked him in the jaw. They headed to the Emergency Room where stitches were put in, though part of his tongue was almost severed. Surprisingly, this same man showed up at the next class, though he didn't have much to say. Afterwards, we never saw him again, which validates Sensei Roald's quote concerning Isshinryu, "Many people will enter these doors, but few will stay."

During the seventies the martial arts were in vogue and a multitude of people were taking up some type of fighting class. Sensei's were opening up dojos, others were making up their own styles, while yet others attempted to teach without having the credentials. It was unfortunate that many people were joining and signing expensive contracts there. Martial arts is about defending yourself and not about getting into a cage to beat your opponent to a pulp. It's about becoming a better person and striving to learn an art that has been passed down for centuries. In reality you are practicing an art that you may never use.

### Detroit Metropolitan Hospital

My first few days working at Detroit Metropolitan Hospital were different. When I went home, I wasn't tired, but I was sleepy from the long drive. I thought that I could live a long life doing this "maintenance stuff." Work was actually fun and not demanding at all. There were pretty women everywhere dressed to impress other women. When one woman left your sight, there was another one to take her place. We had our own lounge supplied with fresh coffee and an environment of 70 degrees. After working there a month another carpenter was hired. His name was Arthur and he was lazy. Had he worked for me, I wouldn't have paid him three dollars per hour to build wood pallets. Arthur never changed a saw blade, even if he cut ceramic tile with a wood blade. The dust was spread everywhere and he just walked away without sweeping. When the lumber truck pulled up with supplies ready to be unloaded, he moved out of the way as fast as I ever saw him move so he didn't have to help.

Our paycheck showed fifty available sick days. This was prorated...after twenty days off an employee may get 80 percent of his or her pay. After thirty days it dropped down to fifty percent until the sick days were all used. Arthur used every one of his sick days, in addition to the paid holidays and vacation time. It gets better...he pulled the "substance abuse card" three times while working with me and he was sent to Belle Hospital for thirty day stints at a time. He visited us by way of the hospital tunnel system wheeling the IV drip stand that was connected to his arm by way of the plastic tubing.

# The Isshinryuist: A Tale of Endurance

We were paid weekly and Arthur sat next to his work bench to balance his check book. Considering we were paid weekly, one might take fifteen minutes to balance a check book. In reality, it took Arthur eight hours (minus his breaks and a nap after lunch) to do so. He had a pencil in his hand calculating the entire time. I considered him to be a smart individual because he was able to get away with this and still hold a job. It was unfortunate that he didn't work with someone else!

The only thing that aroused Arthur from a slumber was the sound of bones (dice) striking something. I always thought of bones as a game of luck, that is, until I saw Arthur throw bones. He took lots of paychecks from employees throwing dice. Sometimes he perspired from playing. Most of the dice-playing was done in the back of our carpenter shop. We were able to keep our door locked at all times because of the thefts that occurred in our area. When the boss knocked, we asked, "Who is it?" We opened the door after he called out his name. This allowed time for the dice game to break up and for people to go back to work for a while. I played dice once and lost each time I rolled.

We listened attentively to Arthur's stories while we had our morning coffee in the lounge while he lay back with his feet out-stretched. He was a good story teller and had some fascinating tales. However, as he told his stories, he started to rub his penis as if he were excited. Nevertheless, we stayed and listened.

# The Isshinryuist: A Tale of Endurance

The hospital was a million square feet of floor space. I learned that most men that worked there carried knives. The knife was positioned next to the wallet with the butt-end of the knife pointing upward. This made for a quick-grab and would easily dissuade an assailant. They were very proficient at opening them in a split second. That is how my brother Gary got cut in the face, by underestimating how fast a knife can be opened with one hand.

Arthur was thin, about six-feet-tall, had a small pot-belly, sported a medium-cropped afro and wore oversized glasses. Even though he was lazy, I thought he was a likeable guy. One morning our supervisor sent us to build some rooms. As Arthur and I walked through the basement we passed various departments; the Morgue, Central Supplies, Receiving, Linen, Security and many others. We were in a group, our carts in a single row and I was leading the way. It seemed like the workers hung out at the entrances to their departments just waiting for someone to talk to. Arthur obliged and had a conversation with each department. I got tired of waiting for him, so I told him that I would meet him there...This was the beginning of our relationship for the next six years. Arthur showed up two hours later, and even less each day after that.

# The Isshinryuist: A Tale of Endurance

One of the nice things about working in a primary black environment was that they didn't tell on each other, or on anyone else for that matter, even if they didn't like you. I never mentioned Arthur's absences either. At least I knew where he was sleeping in case I needed help lifting something heavy. In that case, he had to help or I would have to go to the office for help and he wouldn't want that. When Arthur needed help cutting on the table saw, I immediately gave him a hand. On the contrary, when I needed help cutting, he procrastinated until I had to get help from someone else. After he ignored my requests for help on the table saw, which resulted in little or no help, I decided not to help him either. Arthur asked the Building Operators (B.O.) instead. The B.O.s did light work and assisted the tradesmen, if needed. The saw was powerful and it was capable of throwing things back at you before you could react. It was a spectacle to watch Arthur and the B.O. cut on the table saw. I was hurt by the saw many times and I knew when to run. It was better to take the speeding object in the back than in the front, and, sometimes, there just wasn't time to run. Arthur was aware that the saw was dangerous. I believed that it was safer to cut without the assistance of a B.O. I didn't have to pay attention to what went on because the saw made a distinct sound when trouble was brewing. I simply looked up and it looked up to watch the excitement. There wasn't much time to move before the saw was ready to bite. At first the B.O.s didn't know what was happening, but after seeing that the saw kicked back, they were scared of it, too. We all respected the saw, which required 220 volts with a 208 amp motor to run, with no guard. It seemed as though it just sat there waiting for its next victim. I had been on the receiving end more times than I care to remember, especially cutting plastic laminate. The saw twisted the laminate so quickly that my fingers went numb and bled afterwards.

I started building custom laminate cabinets that fit in the kitchens of the nurses' units. I cut out the sides of the units for the shelves to slide into for strength. I even put in a center brace knowing the nurses would use it as a stepping stool. They were a work of art, with some cabinets still used today. My supervisor wanted to assign another task to me and give the storage units to Arthur and a B.O. By doing so, the work quality was lost. They were still laminated, but the toe-kick was gone, the brace and the cut-outs were lost as well. After Arthur spent six months building these storage units around the hospital, they started to appear in the shop, destroyed.

Arthur never swept the floors, so after a while I never swept his side. He didn't like how different the sides looked and we had a few arguments over sweeping. Everything he brought into the shop remained next to the table saw.

# The Isshinryuist: A Tale of Endurance

It was New Year's Eve, and after having a few brews too many, I looked towards heaven and exclaimed, "Lord, is this all you have for me in life...to clean up after Arthur?" After I talked with God, whenever Arthur brought something down to the shop, I drug it over to his side after he left. Arthur started to get belligerent about the junk on his half of the shop and we constantly argued about the mess. There were doors, hardware, cabinets, and metal framed windows as high as I could pile them. The storage units were heavy and needed two people to be lifted, but I managed by myself. Arthur barely had wiggle room to get into his seat and the dice game had to move elsewhere because of the mess. I used an eight-foot ladder to reach the top of the pile. It happened on a Friday when Arthur was balancing his check book. His side was starting to look like a bonfire. It made a grumble and the cabinets started sliding, which reminded me of ice breaking up on a large river, which makes an eerie sound and you can feel its strength. That was the sound I heard when the cabinets and debris began to topple. Arthur ran, but he didn't make it. One of the cabinets he built landed on his calf and he let out an MF. The check book and pencil flew in the air. His coffee cup was smashed to pieces. I was still laughing as he came over limping and ready to fight, but we only exchanged words.

I had worked at a few places where stealing was a problem, but nothing compared to Detroit Metropolitan Hospital, nothing! I kept my eyes on my tools at all times and listened for the sound of my cart when it was being opened. One of Isshinryu's Principles is, "The ear must listen in all directions." I knew a few heroin addicts that worked within maintenance. Og Mandingo wrote a book named, "The Greatest Salesman in the World," which made me disagree after seeing that the best salesman in the world could actually be a heroin addict, who had the ability to talk a person out of their wife, their kids and their money without making them feel cheated. After my first encounter with a heroin addict, it wasn't long before he had some of my money. This happened a few times until I just said, "No." Most of the time a heroin addict wears long sleeves to cover up the tracks (needle marks). If you shook their hand, it would feel twice the size. A heroin addict doesn't need a fix (shoot up) every day. It takes money...

# The Isshinryuist: A Tale of Endurance

An employee told me about a man who retired from Detroit General Hospital who was the money lender. I was thinking of doing this, and before I even made my decision, hospital workers start coming up to me asking me for money with a guarantee to pay me on Friday. The rate was twenty five cents on the dollar and it didn't matter what day of the week the money was borrowed on. The borrowers thought I was providing an indispensable service. At first I felt bad taking their money, "But it is immoral to let a sucker keep his money, Murphy's Law." I carried a small notebook and pen in my pocket, along with a substantial amount of cash. Even the department directors sought me out to for a quick loan. I kept different dollar denominations handy, which allowed me to complete the loan quickly without drawing attention. I possessed a master key that gave me access to everything, except, pharmacy and administration, so finding a secluded spot was never a problem. On Fridays I spent my breaks and lunch hours looking for people who still owed me. Most of them came up to me with the cash rolled-up in their hand and gave me a handshake: transaction completed. I did a lot of carpentry work for co-workers and they paid me on Friday as well. I was carrying as much as three to four thousand dollars in cash and I didn't want to lose my hard-earned cash to a mugger. There were a lot of people that knew I carried lots of cash. When I carried large sums of money, I put the cash inside my socks and walked on it throughout the day. I never let my closest friends know about this either because "…you never tell the sands what you don't want whispered to the trees, (Khalil Gibran)" You could say that the other mugger was my wife. I had to stash my cash securely because she wanted it and asked many questions, without getting a satisfactory response from me. She used the five "W's" like a good novelist wondering about the money. Without the stashed cash, I would have no working capital to lend.

Arthur had a friend that came into the shop frequently to talk to him. He was a displaced worker from Chrysler that worked as a BO during his layoff. His name was John Jackson. At one time he seemed nice and we would go to lunch as a group. He asked me to laminate his stereo cabinet and I agreed and I drove to his house to pick it up. It was dark when I arrived because of it being winter. John mentioned he had all the laminate and glue for the project. When I got the stereo cabinet out of my van, I realize that it was a piece of junk, which made me wonder if Arthur had built it. It was impossible to laminate it without rebuilding it. It had metal corner braces sticking out that needed to be chiseled out and reset. I decided that I didn't want to do the job because I would have to charge too much to make it profitable. I put the cabinet, along with the glue and the laminate back in my van. Later, I explained to John why I didn't want to do the job. My life changed after that conversation. John was a really big guy and he hated me after this incident. Every time he saw me, he took out his knife and he talked to his friends about how he would like to stick me. Arthur laughed at this and said, "Oh, John," as if he were prompting a showdown. If there was ever a double to John, it would have to be James Edwards, who played for the Detroit Pistons. They were identical in facial features and size. I don't think he cared much for white people to begin with, but now he had a good reason to hate me. I found out later that all the material to be used to laminate the stereo cabinet had been stolen from Detroit Metropolitan Hospital.

The knife he carried looked like a Bowie knife with a hinge; it had a pearl handle and by no means was it street-legal. Every time he saw me, he brandished his knife. I had one advantage, if one may call it that. He used cologne, so I was able to smell him before I saw him. I guess no one ever told him that fragrances are to be discovered, not broadcasted. Arthur, John and I were locked in the carpenter shop quite often. Here he mentioned how he would love to stick me with his knife and I just looked at him and smiled. This made him even angrier, though that wasn't my intention.

I had an arsenal of weapons near me. The power saw was plugged in and sitting on my bench. A couple of pipe clamps were spread around the shop, placed behind scrap pieces of lumber in case I was away from my desk. The nail gun was full, and, if the lever was pulled back, it turned into a machine gun that shot nails. Before the incident with John, I ended up buying a knife with a locking blade. The blade was thin and I sharpened it to the point that when I touched the back of my thumbnail, it stuck. I lubricated the hinge of the knife with three-in-one oil, my favorite lubricant.

I can still see my kids watching me while I practiced opening my knife with a snap of my thumb. I made it an obsession to practice opening it quickly. I became good at it because I don't give up. I was sure that this fool was going to stick me or give it his best shot. I chose the thin blade for the simple fact that I was going to keep it in my rear hand and lunge if needed; the decision was his.

I pictured in my mind how he was going to attack me. I figured he was going to keep his knife in his front hand because this is the way he held it. He was always swinging it as though he was a sword fighter. It must be noted that losing fights while training to be a martial artist is part of the training process and the student mustn't become discouraged, but train harder. In a knife-attack, take the cut on the outside of the forearm because there aren't a lot of vital blood vessels in that area to cause damage like there are on the inside of the arm. I am alert for nine hours a day at work. There were a lot of spots at the hospital where I could be caught alone. I knew for certain that whatever happened, I would have the confidence to handle the situation. This was because I am the type of person who handles all of his own problems without seeking the help of counselors, psychologists and the like. I taught my own children that it is best to always control your mind and not let it control you. However, I am not saying it's a bad thing to seek professional help if needed; I am just explaining how I handle my problems as a martial artist.

Once, I entered the shop with my cart overloaded and struggled with two forty-inch-wide doors that were ten- feet-tall. I had extension cords, tools and wood hanging over the front and back of the cart. I used my foot by way of an extended karate-kick to help me accomplish this feat. In my attempt to get into the shop, the board, which hung over the front of the cart, speared John in the back. He immediately came running around the cart to fight, so I had to remove my foot, which was holding the door open, to enable me to meet him halfway (I always try to shorten the distance for an opponent for a physiological advantage). As I met him, he turned around and went back to talk to Arthur. Shortly after this, John was called back to Chrysler and I put my knife in a drawer for good. I still have the knife because there are memories attached to it. And even though I have found better knives and I have been given better knives...I give them away. My plan to survive working in a hospital was to abide by some principles that I learned from studying martial arts or as Isshinryu instructed me. I set principles for myself: Never get on an elevator if there is a person in it that is wearing a mask; stay away from people who are coughing; treat all work areas as if they are contaminated and never put your hands to your face unless you wash them first. I used my martial arts principles to guide me in all aspects of my life.

## Chuck

My youngest brother Chuck worked with me in Detroit and we needed something from the party store, I asked him to go and wait in line until the store opened. It was a Sunday and the stores opened later. This meant that there would be a lot of people standing in line, with Chuck being the only white person there. I rolled down my truck window and yelled, "If you get into trouble, I will go for help." Chuck sported a natural auburn Afro and had a freckled, boyish face. Whenever he was embarrassed, his entire face turned bright red and this is what happened at the store. I laughed at the sight of him...He probably thought he would be pummeled at the store. He was always game for wrestling and took a number of good throws from me while I studied judo for a few years and became quite proficient at it.

# The Isshinryuist: A Tale of Endurance

The worst day of my life was when my brother, Chuck, whom I dearly loved, died at the age of nineteen. We hung around together whenever possible; we went camping, fishing and hiking several times a year. He also did carpentry work with me. We wrestled a lot and he was just a fun guy to be around. On the other hand, my oldest brother, Craig, was the only one that made it past the age of twenty-eight and he was the brother I liked the least. It seemed like I was burying a brother every two years. I wholeheartedly believe that bad news will find you. I was doing carpentry work on a cottage with a friend. And the only person who knew where I might be was his wife. We didn't have a phone and cell phones weren't around yet. I don't even remember who gave me the bad news; but I was numb when I heard it. I didn't accept the fact that Chuck was deceased until I saw the body. The body was shipped home to Michigan from California, where he was serving in the Coast Guard. His body arrived on my daughter's birthday and we buried him on my son's birthday three days later. During this sad time my children never mentioned their birthdays. They loved Uncle Chuck as well.

Chuck died from alcohol poisoning, which made me quit drinking for some time. Chuck was in the Coast Guard and stationed in California and was celebrating graduating from boot camp. At the PX (Military Store) they sold a hundred and eighty proof liquor, so you can figure out the rest. After the funeral, I cut down a big Mulberry tree and chopped the stump out. I couldn't wait to get home from work to take my frustration out on that tree stump.

Not long after I started working at Belmont Hospital and I was still distraught because of Chuck's death. There was a plumber who worked there named Randal. He was a bully that made fun of people that shouldn't be made fun of, the cruel-type fun. He turned his insults towards me and kept it up for a few weeks. He was about my size but much stronger, he had massive arms and a barrel of a chest. Everyone wanted to be his friend just so they weren't ridiculed by him. Others started joining in "the fun." I was still grieving and they regarded my sadness as cowardliness. They got more daring as time went by and started believing that I was a real wimp. Every day we lined up at the time-clock to punch-out, this included the housekeeping ladies, the kitchen staff, maintenance and others, all waiting in line to go home. Randal started to tease me saying, "You must be the boss's brother because you are both balding." I looked at him and said, "Fuck You, Randal." Every head in that line turned to the next person to recant what I said, until there was no one left to tell. Everyone waited to see what would happen next. Randall was speechless and turned red from anger. I punched out and went home knowing all too well that this was not over yet. Sometimes, to be a man, one must fight.

The same week of the incident, on a Friday, there was a park-party at work. This is where all the hospital workers come out to enjoy beer and food supplied by the hospital. The park was nice and my friend, Gil, ran the grounds. We probably went through three kegs that night. The place was loaded with attractive women. However, they didn't matter to me because I was married; but they were certainly nice to look at. It was a fantastic place to have a party. There was an excellent sound system, a place to dance, a volleyball court, horse-shoes and a bonfire with a continuous five-foot flame. I started drinking and playing volleyball and talking with some girls. Later on, around eighty percent of the partygoers left and this is when the real party began. The drinking helped me forget about Chuck's death. I drank more than I should of because of all the trouble that followed.

It started at the volleyball net with two of my co-workers who hang out with Randal. The alcohol loosened my tongue and it wasn't making me any friends. I saw two of them running towards me wanting to attack me from the other side of the volleyball net (I never told anyone that I study martial arts). I grabbed Sammy as he got close and performed a perfect judo flip on him landing chest-bone to chest-bone. His body made a perfect imprint in the sand, while the sand only touched my toes. If I had been doing a throw for the Olympics, all the judges would have given me a score of ten. The second guy took off after seeing what happened to Sammy. When Sammy got on his feet, sand covered his back from head to toe and he was badly shaken. Come Monday, Sammy goes to the doctor to have his ribs wrapped because they were cracked. Here comes Randal, his arm raised over my head which I took as an aggressive gesture. I flipped him, but I didn't land on him like I did on Sammy. He just got up and laughed it off. We become friends after that. In one night my status changes from being an outcast to becoming another member of the gang.

After the party, I got in my truck and drove away. I was supposed to take the expressway, but thank God I missed the expressway entrance. I drove to the end of Dequindre Road, which seizes to exist at the stop sign. There was another car in front of me, which I ran into; and to make matters worse, I tried to squeeze around both the car and the stop sign causing damage to my vehicle. Then I made a left turn and ended up in the ditch and the truck stalled. Cars began to stop and I thought that I was still going to get away somehow, that is, until someone snatched the keys from me. The Oakland County police showed up and they didn't bother to ask if I was drunk because it was obvious. They gave me a breathalyzer test. I blew so hard on it that I felt like I would pop a blood vessel. I felt that I didn't care, but I did; I just didn't know it yet.

A miraculous event happened next. They dropped me off at a Denny's restaurant on Rochester Road. I went inside Denny's and sat at the counter and ordered breakfast. There was a couple sitting next to me eating and I told them that I would buy their breakfast if they read my ticket to me because my vision was too blurred due to the alcohol. I called my "loving wife" and asked her to pick me up. She said, "No!" and hung up. I then called my parents, who said they were on their way. I waited for them for hours but they never showed up. Denny's management was starting to get upset because I was sleeping at their counter and they kept asking me to leave. I called my friend, Chris, next. He told me he would find me and I knew he would.

The reason my dad couldn't find me was because he went to Denny's in Troy on Rochester Road. I was on the same road but four miles away. I kept sneaking back into Denny's and ordering a coffee to be a patron. When Chris arrives it was about 4:00 a.m. I slept in his car while he drove; he dropped me off at my front door. Everyone was fast asleep inside and I quietly went to bed.

I woke up around 6:30 a.m. and my first thought was, "What, did I do?" My wife started nagging me. "I don't need an enemy, I need a friend," I told her. My main priority now was to find my truck and retrieve it. I called the number on the ticket and I was instructed to come and pick up the truck and bring cash. I remember driving the truck out of the Police Impound with the front-left side looking twisted in a twenty degree angle. While driving, it appeared as though I was always making a left turn when in reality I was going straight. I had fun with this for a few days because cars immediately got out of my way due to my truck's appearance. I still remember seeing my kids, Al and Alysia, looking at me driving my smashed-up truck from their mother's car, a real Kodak moment! The kids rode home with their mom. To my surprise, the traffic ticket I received earlier was only a traffic citation with no DUI. This was a good thing. I drove the truck to work on Monday, two days after the party and when I entered the cafeteria, it seems as though everyone knows. I was embarrassed, to say the least.

There were problems with the insurance company over getting my truck repaired. The argument between the insurance adjustor and me went on for over a month. The tailgate was the only part that didn't need bodywork or paint. I talked to the collision company and asked if the insurance company approved the repairs. The owner of the collision company said that the car insurance company wouldn't even call him back. "Enough is enough," I thought. I called the insurance company on Friday afternoon and left a voicemail stating that if they do not approve the repairs on my truck, I would be waiting on their doorsteps Monday morning. A few minutes later I received a call from the collision owner stating the good news: the truck had been approved for the needed repairs.

With Tammy not picking me up that fateful night caused a lot arguing which led to our divorce. I gave Tammy a thousand dollars for food and other necessities. However, she used the money to hire a smart divorce lawyer. I chose a bad one. My lawyer could have been a double for Jethro Bodine of the Beverly Hillbillies (a sixties sitcom). I wanted her lawyer because he was winning every argument. Tammy was living the good life because I was paying for everything and they still wanted alimony. I even started thinking of making up with her, that is, until one of my friends reminded me that, "As soon as his wife turns the front door knob, she starts telling him what he didn't do." And that is exactly how I felt about Tammy.

# The Isshinryuist: A Tale of Endurance

I met Jethro Bodine at the court house and he didn't seem interested in talking about the case as his eyes were transfixed at something on the ceiling. Though, he looked good in his pinstripe suit. It looked as if someone had put a bowl over his head while cutting his hair. I knew I was screwed. Tammy and her attorney showed up. Mr. Leacock was dressed like a Wall Street attorney. Jethro and Mr. Leacock shook hands and excused themselves. They went to a corner while glancing back at me a few times. Afterwards, they told me that I am supposed to make the house payments, pay alimony and maintain the house. I answered, "You're both fucking nuts." When I said this, Leacock stepped towards me to fight. I moved in to oblige him. Then the courtroom door opened and the clerk told us to quiet down. The noise was interrupting the judge. I told them that, "I am not maintaining the house for anyone. You can put me in jail." We entered the court room and Jethro kept telling me to settle if I knew what was good for me. I told him, "You're supposed to be my lawyer." The judge came in and we all rose. When you don't know a thing about court proceedings, all of this is pretty scary. When Tammy left the stand they asked if I wished to take the stand. I responded, "Do I have to?" They explained that the one who files must take the stand, so I declined. The judge scrutinized the document and asked, "Is there a settlement?" Jethro whispered; "You better settle." "Fuck you," I whispered back. The judge split all the property right down the middle, except for the house furnishings. There will be no maintenance on the house or alimony! I was relieved and I still had my children and they were my priority.

### Carpentry

The last bully I encountered was when I was giving up my carpentry business to move into management. I was hired on a rough carpenter crew. The reason I was able to get top dollar was because I was able to cut stairs, do cornice work (overhangs) and cut rafters. After a day's work, the foreman said that he told the owner that I should get top dollar. Once he told me what my new wage was I didn't have the heart to tell him I had negotiated five dollars more an hour with the owner.

# The Isshinryuist: A Tale of Endurance

We were working in a subdivision building upper-income homes. After a few days, I noticed a twenty-two year old muscular man screaming out orders to everyone on the carpentry crew. He seemed to key in on me because I was quiet. As a rule, I don't try to befriend anyone when starting a new position, I just do my work. He started calling me wrinkle-dick because I was older than him. Additionally, he had a sidekick, the apprentice, who laughed at all of his jokes. After a week I was assigned to do clean-up, which involved going around and fixing mistakes and doing change orders for customers. When there wasn't any clean-up to do I reported back to work with the crew. This idiot was waiting for me to do something wrong. One day he yelled at me at the top of his lungs for not getting the cords out first. The next day he yelled at me for the same thing. I knew it wouldn't be long before we would set things straight. The Great Justice of the Supreme Court, Fred Douglas, once said, "No changes come about without a fight." I was starting to fit in with the crew. This young man was always talking about fighting everyone and he was disliked by most members of the crew. He was laying out walls and he was struggling with dimensions. I politely reminded him, "You add an inch for a bi-fold and two inches for doors." I also mentioned that, "You have been building the same house for three years, it seems like you would be catching on." After this, I knew that our relationship would never improve. When someone starts riding you or talking about your family members, it's time to take a stand, and the knuckles will more than likely be involved. When I went downstairs, the apprentice started to say something and I almost jerked him out of his boots by grabbing his lapels. After one of our breaks, I went back to work and the young man started screaming at me calling me "Wrinkle Dick!" It was beginning to snow heavily. I was standing between some studs on a wall that I was building when I grabbed him and punched him in the cheekbone. He started to fight back, so I hit him in the same spot. He threw a barrage of punches, of which a couple of glancing blows hit me in the forehead. I wanted to throw a knee, but my mind wasn't letting me because I was trapped between the studs and the fight then went to the ground. The young man was on top having the advantage of slugging my ribs through a thick coat and it was starting to hurt. I was just getting ready to throw an open-hand-strike and bring it back with authority using the top of my thumb to attack his groin, but everyone rushed over to break it up. Afterwards, we had lunch in the same room, he was sitting across from me and he was fuming! I was talking to everyone and eating my sandwich while I watched his cheek grow from the punches. When lunch was over, I received a call for a new position and accepted it over the phone. I told everyone that this would be my last day.

The young man wasn't through and a few hours later he came over and told me that I hit like a sissy. I responded by saying, "Call me another name." He left without saying another word. Immediately, I claimed rock-and-roll status among the crew members. The bully had lost the fear-factor that he once held over them. The mistake I made was not hitting him hard enough to finish it. I held back because some people knew that I studied martial arts.

Pontiac

In 1997, I was working at Neighborhood Housing Services in the heart of Pontiac. I was amazed at how hard it was to find my way around. The streets dead-ended everywhere and magically reappeared on the other side of a barricade. I have never been lost so many times in a small city. At this time, MapQuest was becoming popular and I started using it to navigate my way around.

My job was to go to low-income resident homes and gather specifications for new projects. I monitored the work and paid the contractor for their services. We were funded by HUD and there were many stipulations that came with using federal money. The people bidding our work consisted of contractors that were unable to deliver quality work in the real world. They were disappointed when we asked them to sign an eighty page contract. Out of the whole group, there was only one contractor that did tradesman-like work. I understood why the good contractors wouldn't want to do this type of work due to the regulations. Our non-profit also bought dilapidated houses and invested thousands bringing them up to code and resulting in a significant loss when sold. In Pontiac the crack-heads roamed the streets 24/7 looking for anything to steal. They were ready to steal my tools as soon as I turned around and they succeeded. Boy, it was a hazardous place to work.

The next task was to hire minority contractors. The only minority contractor that I found was Georgette, a hot, white girl who was thin, muscular, had great hair and wore shorty-shorts, the kind that expose the bottom of the derriere. I first met her at my office. She was wearing tight blue jeans. When she sat down I noticed something large strapped to her ankle. I asked, "Is that an electronic tether?" She lifted both legs up in the air as though grabbing her big toes. Then she pulled out a knife. I said, "If you lift your legs like that, people will think you have different plans," then I mentioned that the knife should stand upright in her/your back pocket for easy access.

The following morning I arrived at her job site to give her work instructions. Georgette said that one of her co-workers studied martial arts. When I met him he disclosed his lineage. He demonstrated some high-wheeling kicks that he was proud of. Until this moment, he had never heard of Isshinryu. He asked me to show him something. I told him to throw a punch at my head and he did. This only added power to my technique. I hit his arm with an open-hand side-block and slid my hand up grabbing a hold of his trachea and moving it sideways, while lifting him up on his toes (Sensei had done this to me more times than I care to remember). Georgette later confided that I really scared him.

# The Isshinryuist: A Tale of Endurance

The only time I truly feared for my life was when I visited a house where the owner had three full-grown Rottweiler dogs. I was assured that the dogs were chained outdoors. A lady from the office accompanied me and she was extremely religious. I don't remember her name, but I do respect people that take religion to an unprecedented level. When we arrived at the house, a woman in her late sixties with black, graying hair, dressed in a rose-colored nightgown opened the door and greeted us on the porch. I had my camera, the man purse and a tape-measure. After we greeted, I entered the house while my partner waited outside on the porch peering through the screen. I was so involved talking to the homeowner and trying to make a good impression that I forgot one of Isshinryu's principles, "The eye must see all sides." I was in the living room when my eye picked up movement. I turned my head and saw the Rottweiler's. The doorway was over-sized and led into the dining room. They were secured by an extendable baby-gate. They took an immediate liking to me because I was walking-ham. They resembled serpents standing side-by-side as if one continuous body. They got excited and started showing their gum lines and drool was starting to drape around their upper jaw from shaking their head. I forgot about everything, but those dogs. I had ten feet to make it to the stairs. The homeowner was losing control over them. I imagined them sinking their teeth into me while playing tug-of-war with my body. (Yes, I was doing some positive thinking thanks to my past luck with dogs.) The Rotts' pushed the scales at one-hundred and twenty pounds each. A dog has only one objective, and that is to bite you or die trying. I took baby-steps trying to get to the stairs. Once there, I could figure out an escape route. I didn't look at them, but focused on my movement instead. I took another baby-step and another. I felt I was going to make it to the stairs. And then it happened…they sensed their walking-ham was leaving. One of the dogs bit the baby-gate, severing one of the wood segments. Another Rottweiler let out a growl-bark, my heart sank. I didn't run because they may have thought that I was endangering their owner. In my mind I believed all three dogs were airborne. Through my peripheral vision I noticed they were still behind the gate. I made it to the stairs and I kept going slowly and closed the bedroom door behind me. It felt like Christmas in July. I believe that the only thing that saved me that day was the religious lady and her closeness to God.

After gathering my composure I measured the area upstairs that needed improvement. The upstairs bedroom had an entrance door but the stairs were missing and someone could fall. The door wasn't even boarded and it was a drop of fifteen feet. I wanted to jump, but with all the debris scattered below, left me only one escape route and that was to go downstairs and greet the dogs one more time. As soon as they saw me they maintained a fixed-gaze. The worst part was shaking the homeowner's hand goodbye. When I did this, the dogs started to growl in unison like a barbershop quartet. I'm glad this encounter was over and I was happy the religious lady was there or you wouldn't be reading this book.

That night I went to the dojo and Sensei Bufford was the person that I ended up with for a one-on-one kata session. Mr. Bufford studied Isshinryu for decades and he was a fourth Don. I wasn't particularly fond of training with Sensei Bufford because his thought process was bizarre. Bufford was short and had jet-black hair and looked like Moe from the Three Stooges, including the haircut. After watching sensei beat on him for years, I must admit that he was tough. I admire anyone who's willing to stand in front of Sensei Cotton twice a week and take his brutality. I have seen countless students quit after their first encounter with sensei. I told Bufford about my earlier encounter with the dogs. He instructed me on how I should have taken the dogs out and with which technique. I walked away from him and trained by myself. I just wasn't up to his rhetoric tonight. Out of respect I bowed before I left him. Mr. Bufford didn't make anything easy when he taught. On top of that, he would get mad and walk away in the middle of a teaching session.

Atlantic City

It was time for me to leave for Atlantic City for a new job since; I had finished my master's degree from Walsh College. My car was loaded to the max. As I drove away, Wilma (second wife) was the only one waving and crying. She cried because she would have to do the work that I was doing, as well as her own. I have lived in Michigan my entire life, within a thirty mile radius from where I was born. I was excited to go to a different city. When I arrived in Atlantic City it was midnight and pitch-black. But it was exciting to see the casino lights flashing in the darkness with, "Win, and win big."

When I first flew out to Atlantic City, the plane tickets were a hundred dollars. This was what I based my budget on. However, a lot of other states were building casinos and trying to keep the money in their state. After I moved to Atlantic City, air fare doubled, so in order for me to compensate for the price increase, I drove to Philadelphia and took the plane from there while traveling home every other weekend.

# The Isshinryuist: A Tale of Endurance

After arriving in Atlantic City, I noticed that I didn't have anybody. I didn't know anybody here, except the two people that I met while interviewing. I was given an employee orientation and then taken to my office. The two ladies that interviewed me didn't even get out of the car to show me my office. They just gave me the keys and told me to ask someone in the building to show me my new office. They were heading to lunch. They gave me an office directly over the boiler room because they couldn't rent it because it was too hot. It was an empty two bedroom unit with a stove and a fridge. The unit was small, but clean and it was located in a seventeen story high-rise for seniors. This was going to be my new dojo. The floor had tile over cement and it felt as if I had never left the dojo.

After my workday, I pushed my desk back to make room for my katas. I cross trained, too and using a large hill is one the best methods for strengthening legs and knees. I find that walking up hills backwards, sideways and sprinting up, gives one a type of explosive power needed for tennis or kata. The other area that I work on is my feet. I use my toes to pull myself across the room (all strength emanates from the feet).

When I teach self-defense, one of the tactics that I teach women is to be prepared. When I arrive at my office to train late at night I park close to the building. I don't fumble for the right key, the key is ready and in my hand. When out late at night, be especially aware of your surroundings. If a person follows this rule, they won't be left in a position where they have to defend themselves. On many occasions, I have observed women after leaving a store fumbling with their packages in the back seat of their car and oblivious to their surroundings. I teach my students to have their keys ready, open the car door and throw the packages in and then lock the door. Afterwards, she can mess with the packages as long as she wants too. Another self-defense tactic I teach is to have women crawl under the car and hang on to the under carriage for dear life while screaming, "Fire," (Everyone likes to watch a good fire). The word "rape" makes people turn their head and many people are unwilling to get involved.

Atlantic City is one of the biggest sports towns that I have ever lived in. My friends wouldn't take no for an answer when the Philadelphia Eagles were playing. They wanted me to attend their parties and there were sports parties all the time. I befriended one of my maintenance supervisors and socialized with him quite often. Ronnie ran a plumbing business on the side, which could have been full time. He was a likeable guy who had been in prison for a few years for killing a man during a fight. Ronnie boxed for many years. He was big and weighed over two hundred and twenty pounds. Ronnie was always hosting parties for football. His plumbing business was doing well, and his partner ran it full time. The housing authority paycheck was his spending money.

# The Isshinryuist: A Tale of Endurance

After one of his parties he wanted to see some Isshinryu techniques. I did a hand-release and wrenched his wrist pretty hard, to the point where he thought it might be broken. I thought this was a good time to make my exit. As I was leaving, I saw his girlfriend holding his wrist while asking him if he wanted ice or to go to the Emergency Room. We never exchanged Isshinryu ideas again. Ronnie's downfall was his drinking; he drank from the time he got home until he went to bed. After he quit the Housing Authority he had surgery. He was told that if he didn't quit drinking he would surely die. Donald Trump once said, "People work all their lives to attain wealth and then spend all their wealth to attain health."

When I somewhat mastered rollerblades and learned the areas of the city, I rollerbladed through the streets of Atlantic City. I skated by the party store, the one that was a block away from where I lived and a crowd of people hung out there. I gathered enough speed to make it impossible for anyone to catch me on foot. Once they saw me, they yelled, "Get him!" It was always the smallest guy doing the yelling, too. I always changed the time and direction that I rollerbladed by them not giving them a clue until they saw my green helmet flash by them.

The housing authority gave me a company vehicle, a Ford Explorer. Some of my housing sites encompassed four city blocks comprising of nothing, but family housing. Multi-family units are where most of the trouble begins... The hardest part of adjusting to public housing is the fact that it's brighter at night than it is during the day. The weekends that I didn't fly back to Michigan, I worked with my staff on reducing vacancies. There was a lot of crime in Atlantic City. The police went undercover in one of our units, but very few people knew about it, including me. The air was filled with sirens night and day. The police drove on the front lawns of the units at alarming speeds. If someone were to step off of their porch, it could kill them. It was impossible to grow grass between the buildings because of the foot traffic and the police driving on the lawn. There was broken glass everywhere: around the trees, on sidewalks and wherever grass was supposed to be growing. The tennis courts were unusable due to broken liquor bottles. It surprised me that we can put a deposit on beer and soda bottles, but     legislators couldn't fathom putting a deposit on liquor bottles; they were the ones that were busted and strewn all over Atlantic City.

The most interesting part of my day was reading the police report generated by our security department pertaining to the night before. It was faxed to my office before I arrived in the morning. It read like the crime section of a newspaper. My biggest concern while working there pertained to the kids around the age of thirteen. These pre-teens had no respect for life, and because of their size, all matters would be handled with a gun. From my second floor office, I could hear the youth gangs repeatedly talking about "capping some mother fucker" as they walked by. I usually wore a suit and looked like a cop. I broke up a lot of drug deals because of my appearance. As I walked around the corner of a building I saw hundreds in cash being exchanged and as soon as they saw me, they took off. Most of the residents liked to see me around. The kids, on the other hand, knew that I didn't say anything about their drugs. I minded my own business and after a while, I was just a fixture around the housing authority. Though, I never got used to walking around by myself after midnight, which I did quite frequently.

There was a fire at the Housing Authority and the residents gathered around and said that it was a conspiracy and that the housing authority tampered with the wires in an attempt to kill them. I remained in the back of the projects keeping an eye on the unit to stop any looting while maintenance gathered supplies to board up windows. When the maintenance came back, I was told to wait in the front of the building because it wasn't safe. This site was nicknamed little Vietnam. If maintenance made noise in the morning and woke the residents up, they would come out and say that, "If it happens again, we will come out and shoot your asses."

The foundations had crawl-spaces with grates for ventilation. The drug dealers kicked the grates in as soon as we installed new ones. The broken grates allowed rodents to get into the units causing me to hire exterminators. HUD lowered our physical scores, due to the missing grates. Additionally, residents took the batteries from their smoke detectors and used them on their VCRs or other appliances. If these batteries were missing when HUD showed up, this would be another strike against the housing authority. I had my entire staff work to replace missing batteries on 1,700 units. HUD accepted no excuses for this type of violation.

If you saw tennis shoes thrown over electrical wires or tree branches you know that could be a place where you buy drugs. Maintenance cut the shoes off of a tree once and the drug dealers threatened to shoot them if they ever cut the shoes down again. The trash dumpsters posed their own problems for the residents. They were five-foot-tall brick enclosures in u-shape design. At night the residents were so afraid of these areas that when they got close to the dumpster, they swung the bag of trash and ran, I didn't like going over to the trash bins either.

When I left Atlantic City my workers and others throughout the agency use their walkie-talkies to give me the most heart-warming departure. They wished me the best and expressed how much they were going to miss me. The air waves were rifled with heartfelt messages.

## My Teachings

I teach my students, if you get knocked down, you must get up to finish the fight and worry about your injuries later. Sensei reminded me that after the fight, you can shake all you want to. While training with other karate-ka's we used ½ inch diameter dowel-rods that were cut to a length of 18 inches. We pushed the rod below our belly button while walking around the dojo in different directions working carefully not to let the sticks fall. This was difficult to master. If you're reading this book and thinking about studying martial arts, you should consider two things: Are you there to learn how to defend yourself? Or are you here to study the art of Isshinryu and become a dedicated follower? I teach the principles of Isshinryu along with kata and Kuboda. Everything you need to learn is in kata and if you train hard it will let you in on its secrets. After I teach students everything I know about Isshinryu, or that I think I know about Isshinryu, only then will I teach you Mr. Johnson's "S and T" kata which will make you a select few to have been taught his kata.

I remind my students that if you fight, fight with the mind-set that a knife is being pulled on you so you must finish it quickly. A person that holds a knife in his rear hand usually knows how to use it and you should exit. An over confident person will hold the knife in his front hand with the arm extended over their front leg. Many times you can reach over the top edge of the knife and pull it out of his hand. Or you can use one hand to strike the back of the hand while the other hand strikes the inside of the wrist at the same time. This action will send the knife in the air leaving the opponent dumbfounded. But don't stop there, move into combat range, using the eight directions and keeping your feet under your shoulders. Never fight the same line twice. In other words, move!

The most dangerous knife attack occurs when the opponent uses "the claw." I have seen many students look bewildered when confronted with such an attack. Most people freeze and risk losing their life. The claw scenario consists of an opponent coming fast at you and using one hand to knock down anything that you might be using to defend yourself while using the other hand (the one that is wielding the knife) to slash. Both of these strikes come from an overhead position and happen repeatedly. A trained martial artist veers away from this situation, but you will never see him backing away in a straight line. The careful martial artist makes sure to position himself in a place where he hasn't been before.

My favorite knife-defense technique is taught by Mr. Johnson. The finale of his technique ends with your face being smashed in the ground. You experience incredible pain while he laughs at you. The assailant lunges at you with his knife, your leading forearm catches his forearm and you move his arm to the center of your body. This is the first half of the technique. The other forearm takes his arm to the outside of your body this is a hand-off block. The second forearm to touch his forearm should end up with the palm upward and nearly shoulder-high, in a relaxed position. The palm should be relaxed as if holding water. Remember, tension is your enemy. Mr. Johnson described tension as, "He couldn't drive a greased spike up your ass with a five pound sledge hammer."

I reinforce that martial arts cannot be learned from a book, a tape or a movie. It must be done in front of your sensei, a process that takes countless hours and many years to master. It is the only way martial arts can be passed down. Besides, being a committed martial artist, I run and cross-train. At times people ask me, "Don't you find running boring?" My answer is, "No, and you wouldn't either, if you ran faster." When you run, it clears the mind. If you have a problem before you start running, more than likely it is resolved by the time you're finished. In my heyday I was able to run six miles in thirty six minutes. I only ran this speed twice because it was hard on the knees. A runner knows whether it's going to be a superb run after the first three steps. I have run in heat as high as 104 degrees and in frigid temperatures of -40 with wind chill. I ran eighteen years without ever falling. Mud running is my favorite type of running and it is done in the marshes. The marsh scent is incredible and I grew up playing in swamps. The fragrance is a mixture of grasses, poison sumac, lily pads and muck.

A student of mine told that that if a person wants to be become good at something they need to dedicate 10,000 hours towards that endeavor or passion. This equates to three hours a day for ten years. I have surpassed this qualification for training in Isshinryu.

## Judo

After having two kids, I realized all this fighting wasn't conducive to my well-being and it wouldn't help me feed them, if I got hurt. I decided to leave Sensei Roald and quit Isshinryu. Little did I know that Isshinryu would be whispering in my ear... I always did my katas whether I was connected to the dojo or absent from it. A short time later, I heard there was a Judo dojo in Milford and only a few blocks from home. This is where I meet Sensei Wan and when I entered he greeted me enthusiastically. He was a short, stocky man that had studied Judo for decades. Sensei Wan was fourth don in Judo. I signed up and paid for my lessons. I was excited to learn something new. My first randoring (sparing) session was with Sensei Wan. The class was held in a high school gymnasium and I went into the dojo holding onto the belief that, since I was ichi ku (third brown) in Isshinryu that I would excel in Judo, but Sensei Wan proved me wrong. Before we started randoring, Sensei Wan sprinkled baby powder all over the mat, which made my feet slip and slide easily (yes, he was a dirty player).

The best way to describe our first encounter is to compare it to a monkey playing with a snake. Randoring meant that you grabbed your opponent by a lapel and grabbed a sleeve of the GI and try to throw him to the ground followed by a choke-hold, until he taps out (gives up). Mr. Wan taught me how to grab his lapels and we started moving around the mat. I was down, I was up, I was down, and he didn't teach me how to fall and I wasn't hitting the mat softly. If you are going to be thrown, take your fall; it hurts less, and, if you fall correctly, it doesn't hurt at all. In wrestling you are responsible for how your opponent hits the mat; in judo you are responsible for yourself. One of the reasons I am still in the martial arts today is that I can sniff out needless pain.

# The Isshinryuist: A Tale of Endurance

Sensei Wan has us practice a break-fall exercise where he has us run, dive and roll over a few people that are curled   next to each other on the mat. If you touch one of them, you lay next to the person on the far end on your hands and knees with your ribs touching each other. I knew what the end result was going to be. After four people were on the mat, I allowed my foot to drag so I could get in there and be protected from the inevitable... There must have been twelve people crouched on the mats before it happened. The practitioner ran to make the dive and then I heard someone screaming at the end of the pile. He went home and never returned. The guy I feared the most was the one with the two prosthetic legs. I was impressed that he was even able to do judo because of his poor balance. But I figured out his technique when he turned to throw me. He lost his balance and stepped all over my bare feet with his prosthetic legs with sharp edges (One would think they would at least file the edges). After my first encounter, I just dove over him. He thought he was good because of it.

I made a friend at Judo, his name was James Wishbone. He was a brown belt and he was better than his rank implied. Sensei Wan struggled with Wishbone, though he eventually won. Wishbone and I hung out and trained together. He worked with me on techniques, which set me up for a night where I was able to shine in judo. I have more fingers on my hands than the nights where I really shined in martial arts.

Before that, I did some randoring with Wishbone and he threw me. I hung onto him causing him to land on my wrist with my elbow stabbed into the mat. It felt as though he had snapped my wrist. Immediately, I jumped up and bowed out, I ran down the hall where nobody could see me grimacing, I was in excruciating pain. Miraculously, my wrist didn't snap. The incident happened because I didn't take my fall. With Wishbone's encouragement and teachings I was getting pretty good at this "randoring" stuff. I flipped all my friends and it became a common joke to say that, "I will flip you for dinner (literally)."

Whenever I did randoring with Sensei Wan, it was never to my advantage with him being so much better than me. We wore extremely tough gi's that were impossible to rip. Sensei Wan and I are randoring, then he let go with one hand and drew it back over his head which made me wonder what he's going to do with it. I was about to find out first-hand, he slapped me across the cheek as hard as he could and threw me to the mat and proceeded to choke me out. I tapped out to prevent myself from going unconscious. This slap isn't judo! This is just a move used to get the upper hand, like he needed it. No other person has ever done that to me while randoring. Another thing he did was throw his leg between the opponent's legs as they were off balance, which is a proper technique in Judo; but he landed it square against the opponent's groin. The next time, I jumped to avoid his technique before taking his thigh on my groin without a protective cup. The proper technique is that it lands on the inside of the opponent's inner thigh.

# The Isshinryuist: A Tale of Endurance

A guy that had been training in Colorado for the Olympics showed up at our dojo. He didn't rely on underhanded techniques. When I randoried with him, it was a great learning experience. I landed on my rear end so many times that my butt was sore from all the mat exposure. After that, I started tightening up because of from hitting the mat so often. Afterwards, I was airborne over his shoulder, numerous times.

Mr. Wishbone told me about the time when a huge Olympic Roman-Greco wrestler visited the dojo and wanted to wrestle with Sensei Wan. He tried to get out of it by telling him, "We don't do it quite that way here," and then refused to entertain the idea of randoring with him. Wishbone said, "It was funny as hell to see Sensei Wan squirm like that." When Sensei Wan randoried with someone his equal, it was the most boring thing to watch because they were so defensive that they were almost dragging their butts off the mat where neither one can throw each other. Now, how is that going to help in a real street situation? It's important to note that the most important lesson that judo taught me is that you end the altercation before anybody has a chance to put their hands on you.

Sensei Wan refereed a match between an overweight judo practioner and me. He pulled me off balance because of his weight and smashed me to ground, repeatedly, but I didn't quit. I kept getting up and grabbing his gi asking for more. I was taking a real beating and Sensei Wan stopped the session short and made us bow out. I walked away wobbly. My kids came up to the dojo to watch me lose and that is exactly what happened because both of them were crying as I was airborne and hitting the mat repeatedly. Their mother took them home, though I think she would have liked to stay longer to see me get beat.

# The Isshinryuist: A Tale of Endurance

At other times Sensei Wan had us line up about fifteen feet from him and run towards him. He grabbed us by our lapels and let us go when his arm was outstretched above his shoulder. It felt like I was ten feet in the air before hitting the mat and I moved quickly to get out of the way the next person. I didn't want anyone landing on me. We used wrestling mats and they weren't soft. Judo is extremely hard on the knees, and people that have been practicing it for years usually, have bad knees from the grappling, which is a large part of judo.

Mr. Wishbone and I visited the dojo in Brighton. The instructor tried to get some colored belts in the dojo and started promoting students before they were ready. I hadn't been promoted and never gave it another thought. There was a student that joined Sensei Wan's school the same time that I did. When I entered the dojo he was a brown belt. The sensei at this dojo wanted his brown belt to randorie with me. I had no problem with this and we started randoring against each other. The entire class quit working out to watch the match. It was a pretty close match and my opponent's sensei was right next to us yelling out instructions to his student. Neither of us was able to throw each other using defensive moves against offensive and nullifying everything. The instructor continued to yell louder and louder wanting his student to make me tap out. This is what I refer to when I talk about belt color; it doesn't mean a thing on the street.

It is important to "Always over estimate your opponent." My opponent's name was John. John started going at me without any respect for my ability. He wanted this win for his sensei and because he was a higher-ranking student. My moment to shine arrived... In fact, I'm not sure how it even happened, but I threw John and his feet went straight up in the air and his head was level with mine. He hit the mat with the top of his head and all his body weight on top of it. He began to shake violently and he didn't get up. His sensei tried to revive him. After a few moments, he started to come around and the class ended abruptly. He was injured and I felt bad for him. John always respected me afterwards. I randoried with John a few more times; however, I was losing sight of judo because it didn't hold my interest like Isshinryu did. I was still doing my katas, even though I didn't know how to apply them.

Amway

Three things influenced my going back to school. The first was Amway (Soap Salesmen), a costly endeavor. Nevertheless, it got me into the habit of reading and listening to tapes and meeting strangers. After getting a name and number from a person in a grocery store, I would go into my basement and use the phone. It was where nobody could see all the rituals I had to go through to make, what Amway called, a cold contact. Afterwards, I would get an invitation to the prospective client's home to show them the Amway plan. They advised you not to tell your family and friends because, "All they will do is, discourage you from being in the Amway business." In truth, I couldn't wait for my sponsor to leave so I could call all my family and friends, and wished it could be done in one phone call.

After that I was treated as if I had leprosy. It got worse, Tweets (my mother-in-law) was my sponsor. There was no way that Tweets could get up in front of a crowd of people and show the Amway plan. Now of all people, Tweets was my boss, along with Gene, and they thought they were going to get rich because they knew how hard I worked. Gene, Tweets and Tammy went with me when I showed my first Amway plan and I am not even going to rehash the experience. The people didn't join, but I had something to do with it, too. I wasn't very good at presenting or handling all of their negative questions. And it got worse when Charlene started smoking and giving her take on how easy it was to get rich. Gene would say, "You don't need to start a fire under Larry. He is already gone." We traveled around to different states hearing different speakers and how they made it in Amway and the obstacles encountered on their path to riches. The important part of the message was that you could succeed, too. It was like going to church where everybody was friendly for an hour. We spent a couple of days together and ate our meals with these positive people. They were your friends, because after you made that first phone call, you had no other friends.

We went to Atlanta, Georgia in a rented a motor home to reduce costs and it was packed. I brought my group, too; I even sponsored a doctor who wrote a book about banking and I thought I was on my way. I felt the same way when I got my first Publishers Clearing House letter and ran all the way home without opening it only to be disappointed after reading it.

I brought my trusty steel thermos filled with coffee. Wilson didn't know it yet, but he would come dislike my trusty thermos. We had to take turns sleeping because there was only so much room. It was Wilson's turn and I can still picture his face at peace with the world as we passed under the street lights that lit up his face periodically. His hands were folded across his abdomen as though he was lying in his casket. The angelic pose was a Kodak moment. I just filled my coffee cup and laid my thermos above Wilson's head for just a moment. I had plans to move it. And then then the driver hit the brake and the steel thermos was airborne and heading towards his head like a missile. The street light lit up my friends face at the same time. That was all it took. When that thermos hit Wilson's head, I immediately had tears running down my cheeks from laughing. Wilson jumped up, but he was too tall for the ceiling and smacked his head again. Even Wilson's wife was laughing uncontrollably. Everybody was laughing even the driver and he had no idea what had occurred. Wilson tried to compose himself because he had to and I apologized between blurts of laughter.

When we arrived at our destination I was excited to get off the crowded motor home, but I was the last one off and I did a "show-off" type move. There was a cement wall approximately four feet high and about six inches thick where I was about to jump too. I had to duck my head as I jumped and the wall that was four to five feet away. I made a wobbly landing and I was struggling to maintain my balance. When I looked down, it had no other side. It looked as though it was ten thousand feet to the bottom. I was concerned at this point, or to be more truthful, ready to meet my maker. At this point, fate just had to play itself out. Suddenly, Fred yanked me off the ledge. I definitely used one of my nine lives on that one. The cliché, look before you leap stuck in my head after that incident.

Amway definitely wasn't going well for me and I can actually say that it was making me poorer than I have ever been because I wasn't doing carpentry work on the side. Charlene and Gene weren't doing anything with their Amway business and were hoping to become rich off my efforts. I tried to motivate my group and paid $600 for a set of pans. The Amway pans put me in the thousand dollar club. My group quit the next month. If they would have quit the month before I wouldn't have bought those over-priced pans.

I went over to Louis Egger's house. He was a carpenter and a friend that I worked with while doing rough carpentry. Louis was a fun soul who always had weed and good weed at that. Tammy acted as though she was my boss and she sure could fuss. I would do anything not to hear her fuss. And she put her foot down on weed. I would work for free just to get away from her fussing; she was relentless. Louis was fun to hang around with and he had money because he would sell herb, his wife worked full-time with no kids. I was married at nineteen and never had a chance to fulfill the wild side of me. The first thing Louis and I did when I arrived was smoke some of his good herb. A friend with weed is a friend indeed. Louis thieved a whole house by piece or pile, if he had the choice. It was stacked in piles with tarps over them protecting them from the elements on his ten acres. He figured out how to build a beautiful ranch with the windows, doors, furnace and whatever else he got his hands on. He had to buy some stuff, but for the most part he stole the whole house.

It was extremely cold that morning and we were going to shingle his house. The coldest part of the day for Michigan winters is when the sun comes up and crystalizes everything. I grabbed a home-made ladder that Louis built. It was made of 2*4's and it had a platform on top that you could stand on to finish the overhangs. It had a notch where you could stick the platform against the outside corner of the house where it wouldn't slip and fall over. The platform kept you far enough away from the building to work on the overhang comfortably.

# The Isshinryuist: A Tale of Endurance

Louis thought I was taking too long to set up the ladder and started yelling that I worry too much. Louis was always yelling about something, but in a fun way. I was concerned about ladders because I have fallen from them more than once. When you fall from a ladder it's over before you know it and then it's a healing process. Gravity only gives you one chance. My job was to stop the ladder from moving that first inch. The best way to accomplish this is to throw a bundle of shingles to keep it from sliding or a screwdriver pushed up tight to the leg of the ladder. Louis was still yelling that I worried too much and we were both high and laughing. When I got on the roof it was frosted. It had a 7/12 pitch which meant that every foot of distance the rise of the roof is seven inches and anything over a 4/12 causes concern. I made it across the roof with caution and got a few shingles nailed down which made it safe and frost free. Louis grabbed the ladder and is still yelling, "You worry too much." I was looking over the peak of the roof. Louis was leaning the ladder against the house telling me that I didn't need a bundle of shingles because it took too much time. He tried to step from the platform onto the roof. The ladder slipped. He didn't go down immediately because he grabbed a limb that was hanging over the house, but the branch was only ¾ inches in diameter thick. Our eyes met for a second and the Frenette curse went into effect. I was laughing and he hadn't even fallen yet. He wiggled the branch back and forth a couple of times and my eyes zeroed in on the branch. It was splitting apart and our eyes met for a second time and then, Louis was gone.

I quit laughing. I was ready to save my friend. I yelled, "Louis, are you all right?" No answer. Again, I yelled, "Louis, are you alright?" No response. I had no way down because the roof was iced over and it was a fourteen foot drop on frozen ground with construction debris everywhere. I listened, but I didn't hear anything. I looked down at a 4' *8' sheet of plywood and pulled out my nail-puller. Every carpenter carries one in his pouch. It eases the nail-head out of whatever it is burrowed into, allowing you to grab it with your hammer afterwards for easy removal. I tried to get an answer out of Louis, but not a peep came from the corner of the house where he fell. I figured there were sixty-four nails in a sheet of plywood. I was busier than a cat in a litter box trying to save my friend. When I got two-thirds of the nails removed I used my strength to finish the task. I yelled one more time, "Louis, are you okay?" This time he answers, "No." When I made it over to him, he was lying face down and his forehead was still lying on the rock. There was a pool of blood that had saturated the snow. I immediately checked to see if the rock was okay (just kidding). I helped Louis to his feet and we headed to the doctor's office. Louis was in there a long time. When I went to see what was taking so long, I saw several people hovering over his head while his feet wiggled back and forth. I figured they were almost done and he received ten stiches from the ordeal. Afterwards, Louis treated me to breakfast and we headed back to his apartment. The workday was over. After we smoked his herb I noticed a giant poster with W.C. Fields on it with a caption that read, "If you try something once and fail and try it again and fail, then quit. Don't be a damn fool about it." From that moment on I quit Amway and it was because of the W.C. Fields poster.

My second influence for going back to school was Rick Seger. He just hired in at Detroit Metropolitan Hospital and had recently, finished his Electrical Engineering Degree at Lawrence Technical University. At the time I was doing Ride-Share with Tom Perry who worked for HUD. After riding with Tom, I truly believe that God takes care of fools and babies. Our first drive together went smoothly because I was driving. I picked him up and I let him off without incident. Tom was quite heavy, or you could say obese, but I enjoyed his company. But after the first day, with Tom driving, I realized I was never going to sleep while Tom was at the wheel. When I picked him up he smelled of something that most people wouldn't think to eat for breakfast, like pizza or fish. We would talk for a while then Tom fell asleep before we arrived at the McNamara Federal Building in Detroit. He would sleep with his head leaned back and his mouth wide open and it sounded as though it was starting to fill up with fluids the longer I drove. He was making a loud gurgling sound. Tom was out like a light and I decided to have some fun. As I approached the Federal Building I would make wide turns, so as not to wake him up, and when we were in front of the federal building I would yell, "Wake up Tom. We're here." He was disoriented and trying to grab all his stuff and he always had a huge briefcase with lots of papers that he took to and from work. Tom struggled to get out the car because of his weight, along with everything else he was carrying. One time he got out and lost all of his papers in thirty mile an hour winds. I watched him as I pulled away and it didn't look like he was being very successful at retrieving them. Another time, Tom closed his tan trench coat in the car door. That was the fastest I have ever seen him move and he was going sideways while beating on the window frantically for me to stop. All this was mild in comparison to what I endured with Tom at the wheel.

# The Isshinryuist: A Tale of Endurance

Tom arrived in his an orange Fiesta; it was one of the smallest cars I have ever been in. The windshield was so close that you could stick your tongue out and touch it. Not many amusement rides scare me, but riding with Tom was more than an adventure. At first, I gave him the benefit of the doubt, but not for long. It started out with me saying, "Tom, you need to hit your brakes. After a while I would use my hand on the dash as though I was training Pavlov's dog and it was working. He would hear my fingers slap the dash and then he would apply the brake. The Lodge Freeway was white knuckle driving, even when I was at the wheel. We would hit pot holes so large that they would almost swallow up his car and he would wonder what happened afterwards. Once, there was a big chain strewn across our lane. You could see it from a quarter mile away. I thought that there was no way that he was going to run over it because he had plenty of time to change lanes. When we hit that chain it sounded like it tore the bottom of the car apart and Tom asked, "What was that?" I answered, "I think it was a chain." He wanted to sell me his car and I was thinking I would never buy something that he had driven even once. We had so many close calls while Tom drove, that I grabbed the steering wheel four times from him. Yes, four times! Just think how many times you have ever grabbed the steering wheel from someone. The drive home was worse because the sun would shine through the window making Tom sleepy. When he started rubbing his head and scratching his leg, it meant he was ready to nod out. This was double duty for me because I had to watch all lanes of traffic and I had to wake Tom up as well. When I woke him up he apologized and said, "It's my new medicine that's making me fall asleep. That was enough for me. My heart couldn't handle it anymore. I told Tom that they put me on afternoons for a while trying not to hurt his feelings. I did like him and he was a great conversationalist, but he couldn't drive.

# The Isshinryuist: A Tale of Endurance

The other influence I mentioned that got me back in school was my new friend, Rick Seger, who was about my height and was an avid weight-lifter and lifted four times a week. He lived in Howell, MI again, it was on the way to the hospital and this enabled us to share rides. Rick had a new car, dressed impeccably and was groomed to go places in the corporation. Even though he lifted weights and had large arms, for some reason, they still called him little Rick at work. I would tell him that, "You can't forget to strengthen those hands. They are the life blood to any workout." I have stopped many aggressive wannabes just because they had a chance to shake my hand first. It has been proven that lifting weights or strength-conditioning improves the physical performance of any athlete. I don't do much weight lifting, but I do strengthening exercises. Pushups are the main staple of my workouts. Lately, I have added chin-ups and pull-ups to my regime, especially after finding out how weak I was from not using these muscle groups for years. There are times when I eliminate all strengthening exercises in my workout regime. This allowed me to focus on my Isshinryu technique alone. If I am doing my Isshinryu correctly, I shouldn't need strength to defeat my opponent. If Isshinryu is practiced in the fashion it was designed, a ninety pound woman should have the same effect on a person as Shimabuku.

# The Isshinryuist: A Tale of Endurance

Rick and I were about the same age and we both had two kids. He was married to a Japanese lady whom he met while in the Navy and he served in Vietnam on a PT boat. When his wife called his name, she would call him, "Licki" because she couldn't pronounce the R's. His dad left him at a young age, just as my mother left me when I was three-years-old. Rick told me the story of his dad coming over to pick him and his brother up on a Friday night. They would pack their suitcases as soon as they got home from school and drag them to edge of the driveway waiting for their dad to show up. Their mother would yell out and tell them it was getting dark. They would respond, "Just a little longer mom. We know he's coming." He would never show because he was an alcoholic. This formed an incredible kinship between us for the next few years.

Rick and I stopped for a beer after work. Rick called his wife and told her that he was going to be late, but I knew better than to call Tammy. While Rick talked to his wife he was leaning against one of those short, brown phone booths mounted outside the bar. He threw a kick at my groin. I simply moved to where I wasn't and swept the remaining leg out from under him. He went down and you could hear his vertebras sliding across the laminate edge of the phone booth. The back of his head hit the shelf and for the finale, his butt hit the marble floor and he was stunned. The phone was hanging by its chrome phone cord and twirling in mid-air. Rick's wife was yelling, "Licki, are you there? What's the matter?" He answered and afterwards, we laughed it off. We decided on the South Lyon bar for our next stop. It's a red neck place and I knew a lot of people there from sparring with them in my brother's basement.

# The Isshinryuist: A Tale of Endurance

Our new destination was twenty minutes down the road. At the stop light I inadvertently cut-off another driver. We laughed it off and kept driving. The other driver wasn't so forgiving and starts tailing us and giving us the F-U sign. He is riding our bumper and honking his horn as well. I showed Rick my trick and that was to take two wheels off the road, so it sprays gravel, making the driver back off instantly. We started laughing and the guy could see us laughing. He passes us and afterwards, he slows down and started yelling giving us his IQ sign. Rick was taking off his seat belt and getting ready to fight. I told Rick that I had another trick and I started pointing my finger to the side of the road as if saying, "Let's pull over and fight." The little pickup pulled off the road and we kept driving. The dude was madder than a wet hen and he passed us again. This time he got in front of us and he was going slow, so slow, that the traffic was backing up, twenty cars deep in a rural setting and he's not falling for that pull over and fight stunt, again. Remember, you cannot get someone out of a car, if they don't want too. From the other direction a patrol car passes and sees the backup. He turns around and our adversary starts driving fast. The cop is coming fast and the little pickup is trying to get away. He pulled into the parking lot of the South Lyon Bar. As we pulled in, he was running by us. He yelled at us, as he disappeared in the crowd. When we went inside he was waiting for us and ready to fight. I talked him out of it and he bought us a beer. Rick asked, "How did you do that?" I said, "Nobody will punch a smiling man."

### Shodan

Isshinryu has always taught me to think in principles. While following your passion there will always be things pulling you away from it and that is called, "Life." It's your job to find a way around these obstacles to become a martial artist or whatever your heart holds dear, as your destiny. I read the book "Passages" and I agree with the book's premise that people are in your life to help you pass from one stage of your life to another. And that you should realize the time spent with them was a gift. When a relationship or friendship is over, be thankful...The only woman that I can count on for guidance and protection is "Mitzi Gami," the woman on my Isshinryu patch. She's been with me through good and bad times. I received my Shodan Belt while married to Wilma, but I never regretted missing the previous opportunities to attain it. Maybe it was Mitzi Gami that led me in a different direction. I was a brown belt for seventeen years. This fact is unimportant because I am not in martial arts for rank.

# The Isshinryuist: A Tale of Endurance

I informed Sensei Cotton that I was accepting a job offer in Atlantic City. That night I heard him whisper to Sensei Telfa, "I want you to line-up with Frenette and work him over." Sensei Telfa lined up in front of me and I knew it was show time. Sensei Telfa was a fourth don who trained under Sensei Cotton. When he led class, we all felt our muscles burn. Sensei Telfa was about 6'2" with little body fat. He recalled the time an altercation was about to unfold where he was out-numbered four to one. What stopped the altercation was when he yelled, "I will fight all you Fuckers at once!" I have only seen two people put fear in the eyes of Sensei Telfa; Mr. Johnson and Sensei Cotton, and I don't blame him. We were discouraged when Sensei looked at his hands saying, "Look at all the Ki (energy) flowing from my hands." His Ki covered the palm of the hands with little white dots. Sensei was able to put energy into our bodies through bunkai, though he warned us not to go home with energy still flowing inside us. I wish I would have known sooner. Sensei taught me to accept the energy as I was taking a hard strike. By following his teachings, I am amazed that I was able to take some of these hits. I only share this type of knowledge with a student that trains with me for many years.

Based on Mr. Johnson's teaching, we don't spar and he refers to this as down-training. We practiced one-step kumite (fighting). This is where your opponent punches or kicks; afterwards you block and strike his body with a kick or a punch. You can't avoid the retaliatory punch or kick and it's evident who the better karat-ka is.

When Sensei Telfa attacked, I countered with a punch. I didn't hit him hard, but with enough force that he knew I hit him. It was Sensei Telfa's' turn to attack, and it seemed like he listened to Sensei's instructions. After going back and forth several times, it hurt. I was matching Sensei Telfa's power as we punched each other in the chest. Sensei Telfa says "Let's lighten up before we both suffer injuries." I agreed. When sensei walked by and asked how we were doing, Sensei Telfa told him, "We are beating the crap out of each other." He walked away smiling.

Sensei Cotton was one of the few sensei's that I wanted to be promoted under; this gave me the blood line I was looking for, a first-generation student of Sensei Cotton, a second-generation student of Mr. Johnson and third-generation student of Tatsuto Shimabuku. It is an impressive blood line. I worked out for decades to acquire the knowledge from their teachings.

# The Isshinryuist: A Tale of Endurance

After decades of training and learning the art of Isshinryu, Sensei promoted me to Shodan. Isshinryu is an art that can be practiced for a lifetime, but hopefully, you will never need to use it to defend yourself. It is an art that leads to strength, confidence and health and it also enhances other areas of your life. Sensei has me line-up in front him and the other Shodan's. He asks me to remove my treasured brown belt, which has been such a part of me. Sensei hands me a crisp, black belt that isn't soft and comfortable like my brown belt. I accept the belt graciously and he instructs me to put it on. Out of respect, I turn around and face the Ku's (lower belts) before putting on my new belt. Out of respect you never tie your belt in front of anyone, especially, in front of sensei. When sensei promotes students, he never charges for the promotion or the belt. Achieving a new rank is not considered a big deal. There is no formal beating or ceremony. Sensei believes that you are tested every time you show up at his dojo.

Sensei informs everyone that I will be starting a new job in Atlantic City. He goes on to acknowledge that I have studied Isshinryu many years and that I am his Sempi (He who came first). He also mentions he needed to promote me in case I start working out with someone in New Jersey. Then the new sensei would lay claim to me if he promoted me to Shodan. He also said that, "When I go into the new dojo, I will probably kick the instructor's butt." I am touched by these words and I was trying to fight back a tear. I have only felt this type of emotion a few times in my life: when my kids were born and when I finished my master's degree.

After the promotion, I smiled broadly and pictures were taken of this festive occasion. I walked over to the stage, where sensei changes. The stage was a raised platform that included two steps. The area was 8' * 8,' with the same 12"*12" tiles, but no concrete under it. It had a table and two scratched folding-chairs and a low suspended ceiling. I had trained here for over twenty years and this was my first time walking on the stage, which is considered sacred ground. I knew that when this was over I would be given a major beating and it would happen within two weeks. I showed Wilma, my black belt, she was proud of me. I let my son know that I was a black-belt. I returned to class sporting my new black belt and I lined up with Sensei and the other Shodan's. My black belt looked like it had wings because it was so stiff. After the bow in and exercises, the higher ranks worked with the lower ku's.

You can't quit working out because of an injury or you will never become the karate-ka or the athlete you set out to be. When playing racquetball, a friend didn't want to play me because I had a knee injury. I was actually dragging one of my legs. I told him that if he forfeited the game, I would move up to his level and he would drop down to mine. He reluctantly played and won the best two out of three matches. When I am too sick to train, I walk at least twenty minutes and this gives me the momentum to train. I believe in cross-training because it benefits my Isshinryu. I prefer sports or games with an object to hit, like tennis.

# The Isshinryuist: A Tale of Endurance

We finished our workout, I went home unscathed. Sensei didn't even lay his hands on me. I have three more workouts before moving. To avoid a beating, I could call Sensei and tell him that I have too many items to complete and I couldn't attend anymore workouts. But, I know myself and I show up for class on Thursday. There was no beating for my Shodan rank, so something seemed amiss. But on Tuesday, with two classes left, Sensei had us line up for one-step kumite and he lined up in front me. I wondered if he was worried that I'd hurt him; I quickly dismissed the thought. I took some aspirin beforehand because I knew this was going to hurt. My strategy was to eat aspirin before every class until I left for Atlantic City. I was glad there wasn't an audience for the beating. Sensei threw the first kick and I blocked it with my forearm. I was taking it easy on him and hoping that he would go lightly on me. I didn't have a lot options, but let's err on the side of caution. It was Sensei's turn to block my leg and counter. I threw a kick and he didn't even counter with a punch, but he didn't have too. He knuckle-blocked my shin and I jumped around because I couldn't stand on my leg. This was one of the major premises I learned from Mr. Johnson. If an opponent strikes, you take out their leg or arm. It is easier to fight a three-pegged person; there are multiple places to strike on the legs or arms. Sensei did a few more knuckle-blocks on my shins. We moved on to the upper body kumite, middle blocks. He told me to go first. This way I had no idea of how much power to put on my punches. Again, I erred on the side of caution because he can end this contest with one strike. Sensei was throwing punches at full-speed and I was intercepting them easily with an executed punch moving up and down his body. It was his turn: he blocked my punch and landed a thunderous punch to the right side of chest where I could feel the imprint of his two big knuckles (Urakine). To avoid long-term injuries when practicing, we punch the right side of the chest because the heart is on the left. We do this ten times on each side to each other and then go through open-hand strikes with a punch. I let him have some pretty decent punches. And I was working on his nipples, filleting them in different directions and stretching them. I was trying to do it in a way that he didn't realize what I was doing, so he didn't start attacking my nipples. There are many nerve endings located directly behind the nipples which makes it very sensitive. I wasn't winning this match, and, if I were leading the class, we would go and do something else. I have never won any battles against any of my Sensei's. It was easier to concede, or, better yet, to cower. We moved into head-punches and I was very attentive because he could knock me out or shatter my face if I didn't block his punches. Sensei threw them with full power. He made me forget about my bills and any other distractions. I knew that I would never encounter a tougher opponent on the streets than Sensei. He started stutter-stepping (changing speeds) while throwing his punches and trying to fool me. I was blocking and countering well. This is where I messed up and why I did it, I will never know. On an overhead block, I wiggled my fingers to show Sensei that I was loose. This infuriated him as we moved into exercise number ten, which was a block taken back alongside the ear followed with a punch to the chest. He changed the counter to drop the little knuckle of his fist to the less fleshy part of my breasts. He had my full attention and my chest was feeling the pain. When we finished, I walk away as if nothing hurt. In reality, I could barely throw a punch because my legs, chest, ribs, shins, arms and organs have been brutalized. Sensei knew what he had done to my body. I had fifteen more minutes before the end of class and I had to keep up the façade that I wasn't in pain, but everyone in class knew I was hurt.

# The Isshinryuist: A Tale of Endurance

When I arrived home, Wilma was accompanied by her parents and was getting out of the car. I moved from the garage to the house like a curled rat. I heard Wilma telling her parents in a loud voice that I was really hurt this time. I continued to maintain the façade that I was fine. It was nice to get to the bedroom to assess the damage, though everything was too sore to touch. Wilma asked me to quit "this stuff" because it will come back to haunt me in old age in the form of arthritis. I thought that she was right this time.

When I returned to class on Tuesday, Sensei Cotton didn't make us go through basics or calisthenics. He told us that he would be around to check us out. This meant that we worked on kata for two hours. There were two mirrors in the dojo and they were always in high-demand. If you are practicing martial arts there isn't a better tool that I can recommend. You can see your mistakes while practicing. Don't forget to turn sideways while breaking down your katas and to see if you're standing up straight. I was using the mirrors to check my form, delivering three consecutive elbows, the way Mr. Johnson taught Sensei Cotton. The elbows follow natural body movements. Remember, tension is your enemy, if you feel tension, you are doing something incorrectly. After the beating I was doing kata in the mirror. Sensei walked up to me and made a gesture to punch me in the chest. I tightened, preparing my body for the strike. He knew I was sore and was trying to scare me and it worked.

Everyone lined up and bowed-in before and after break. We used our break as we pleased, but most of us continued to work on kata. I talked to Rita, sensei's wife. She confided in me that sensei walked around the house pulling on the front of his t-shirt to avoid it rubbing against his nipples while yelling "Fucking Frenette!" His nipples bothered him all weekend. I gathered some satisfaction after hearing about this.

Wilma

I have an A-type personality trying to stuff more into a day than time allows. I wake up every day as if I were in the military. (When a new girl entered my life I told her that she was about to get the least amount of sleep she had ever gotten.) I read a book titled, "How to Sleep Less and Live More." I was able to cut my sleeping requirements to five hours a night. I kept up this ritual until I married my second wife, Wilma. She was good looking and had legs like Angie Dickinson (actor). Nature also favored her with a wine-glass-ass, the kind that is common among black women, but unusual for a white girl. I use the term wine glass because, if you set a wine glass on her ass, it wouldn't fall off. She had thick, dishwater-brown hair and hazel eyes. She dressed on the trashy side, which I liked. I often heard men making comments about her legs. She had three children and we all got along, until I married her. I first met Wilma's son, Butch when he was nine-years-old. He started throwing kicks and punches at me and I landed a couple of light kicks on his breast bone. He said, "Your Kung Fu is better than mine," I chuckled.

Shortly, after Wilma and I married, I spent less than a week with her before going to Upstate New York for a five-day, all-expenses paid American Management Association (AMA) seminar. I wrote a three-page essay of what management meant to me. The first night there, while sitting around the campfire, the man in charge of the camp went over the rules stating, "We cannot consume alcohol or drugs on campus." He turned his back and instructed us to leave any of these substances on the ground. We all laughed and when he turned around, there was nothing there, but plenty of laughter. We slept in cabins close to the lake. We had a talent show and I did Seisan kata. We went water skiing and played b-ball when the management sessions were over. We had speakers come in from all over the country to give us lessons on management. I retained The Code of Ethics and use it to this day, "If you don't want your friends, family or relatives to see it in the paper, then don't do it."

When I returned home, I learned that Wilma's father, Zud, had attempted suicide by shooting himself. "This is great," I thought. I finally rid myself of the Pilson's and now I had to deal with this. Wilma and I both worked for Belmont Hospital. Wilma's family gathered in their cry room waiting to hear about Zud's fate. Sally, Zud's wife, took center stage screaming, yelling and crying. She was extremely graphic telling us about the blood splatter from the attempted suicide. Everyone was crying. Wilma and I went over to her parent's house to clean up the mess. After Sally's graphic description, I was prepared for the worst. We entered the house and looked around, but we didn't see the horrific scene described by Sally. There was one spot of blood the size of a dime spattered on the white linoleum floor, Wilma cleaned it up with one tissue. I liked Sally and she was funny. Zud shot himself in the mouth with a twenty-five caliber pistol. The bullet bounced off some dental work lodging the bullet near his spine where the doctors were afraid to remove it. Zud never smoked or drank, and now he walked like Boris Karloff in the movie "The Mummy." The moral of the story if you want to kill yourself put the gun up against your eye where there's nothing to stop it.

# The Isshinryuist: A Tale of Endurance

During a family gathering my uncle saw Zud wearing a neck brace and exclaimed, "Great lawsuit. Did you get any money?" I headed for the bathroom and waited for this to be over. I always checked to see what Zud had in his hands when he entered our home. I was ready to confiscate it or take off. I wasn't a blood relative and highly expendable. Sally was instrumental in helping Zud get over his mental problems. When they argued, she would roll her finger around her ear insinuating that he was crazy. When Zud saw his psychiatrist, he told the doctor about Sally's actions. Sally was in the waiting room and was asked to step into the doctor's office to be reprimanded. Afterwards, Zud tried to prove he still had all his facilities. He tried to ride a bike and got hit by a car, which landed him in the hospital. He got hit by a second car on an expressway ramp and lived. Years later, I asked my son if he thought Zud was still alive. He said, "Anyone who is that much of a burden is surely alive."

Mr. Johnson

I have been doing martial arts for nearly forty years and Mr. Johnson was the best practioner that I have ever known (period). I never called Mr. Johnson sensei because he never let us call him sensei and I wasn't about to buck tradition after seeing what level that he could bring martial arts too. If you wanted to upset him just call him, "Master" When Mr. Johnson did bunkai, it felt like dynamite going off inside your body. As soon as he hit, I broke out in a sweat. When he was doing bunkai on a student, another young student asked, "Doesn't that hurt?" Mr. Johnson replied, "Isshinryu is a lot like life, it hurts sometimes."

A man came into Mr. Johnson's dojo and said, "I want to learn self-defense." Mr. Johnson asked, "Why do you want to learn martial arts?" The man answered, "I want to learn how to defend myself." Mr. Johnson responded, "Sir, based on the pain that I am going to inflict on you, you'd be better off going to your local hardware and buying a shotgun." I think this is why (my) sensei hurts new students in the early stages of training to see if they are going to stay around.

I attended a seminar taught by Mr. Johnson. Sensei Shin was present and watched me do a kata. He made some changes to my kata and said, "Kata tell story." Afterwards, he punched me in the chest and it hurt. I thanked him and bowed for his knowledge. Sensei Shin was an eighth don who had a dojo in Washington State. Even though he was eighty-years-old, he could do pushups with his arms stretched out in front of his head, he was a phenomenal physical specimen.

# The Isshinryuist: A Tale of Endurance

Everyone gathered around Mr. Johnson as he explained how to break down kata into bunkai. He mentioned sensei Shin's name. He thought that Mr. Johnson was going to use him for his Uke and Sensei Shin immediately told Mr. Johnson, "Me too old, me too old!" Mr. Johnson explained, "I'm not going to hit you." I know how he felt because I feel the same way, though I am not that old. Mr. Johnson hit me in the arm with only two inches of air between my arm and the bottom of his fist, I fell to my knees. He did it again, only this time he waved his other arm under my forearm and then smacked me in the same spot. I stayed down a little longer than the last time, as he chuckled. When the seminar ended, I couldn't use my injured arm to drive from Jackson to Manistee, Michigan to meet up with friends for fly-fishing. I didn't tell anyone what happened to my arm because I knew they wouldn't believe me.

Sensei Amstar was Sensei Cotton's number one student, he informed me that I wasn't allowed to attend Friday night's excursion. During this time Sensei Amstar was a follower of Mr. Johnson and he took Isshinryu seriously. He was a small gentleman who probably disliked me because, in the past, I used to beat on him when we spared bare-knuckles and he still remembered those sessions. That was before he started following Mr. Johnson.

Sensei Amstar was now my superior at the dojo. He was an ass most of the time; he could get away with it because he was good at Isshinryu. I remember watching Sensei Cotton beat on him for years and I was glad he was here because of it. Sensei Cotton usually beat on his top students until they quit and never spoke to him again.

# The Isshinryuist: A Tale of Endurance

At one time I was training in two dojos with Sensei Blate and Sensei Cotton. Sensei Blate allowed me to call him sensei, which was rare, because you don't train with more than one sensei. During this period, I established a type of hierarchy system between the two dojos. Sensei Blate was the undisputed top dog followed by Sensei Cotton. I was working out at Sensei Blate's dojo the night before Mr. Johnson's seminar and I wanted to meet him. Earlier Sensei Amstar told me that I couldn't attend the Friday night seminar. My thought was forget what Sensei Amstar said about me not being allowed to attend the seminar. I knew that if I attended, I would have to pay for it later. While at the dojo I observed Sensei Blate doing a kata. In a respectful manner, with my hands to my side and showing the utmost respect, I patiently waited until he was done. I asked him if it was ok for me to attend the seminar and pay the fee. Sensei Blate looked at me and said, "Yeah, Frenette. Just tell them you are with me." I could tell he liked me. I was excited that I was finally going to meet Mr. Johnson. I went home and washed and ironed my gi. The next evening when I entered the seminar, Sensei Amstar came running in my direction and told me that I wasn't allowed to be there because of my rank.

At this point Amstar was almost growling while telling me that I couldn't attend Mr. Johnson's seminar for Shodan's. I played my trump card and told him that Sensei Blate invited me. He reeled his chest back and didn't say another word. Few people would want to tangle with Sensei Blate and I couldn't help, but smile. I was offered a black belt over ten years ago, but I declined the promotion. I am not in Isshinryu for prestige. Sensei Cotton told us a story about his two cats and how one of them always beat on the other, until one day, the other cat took top spot because he was no longer a kitten. This is what keeps me working out in Isshinryu. I want to be that top dog and I strive for that top spot.

# The Isshinryuist: A Tale of Endurance

We are grateful to Sensei Blate for finding Mr. Johnson; otherwise, we'd still be doing athleticism workouts. Shimabuku able to toss around those Jar Heads (Marines) in Okinawa without much effort, in spite of weighing a little over a hundred pounds by using the "Eight Isshinryu Principles" by Kenpo Gokul:

1. A person's heart is the same as heaven and earth.
2. The blood circulating is similar to the sun and moon.
3. The manner of drinking is either soft or hard.
4. A person's unbalance is the same as unwanted weight.
5. The body must be able to change direction at any time.
6. The time to strike is when opportunity presents itself.
7. The eye must see all sides.
8. The ears must listen in all directions.

There is more to martial arts than brute strength; it is an ancient art that has been passed down for centuries. At the seminar all the high ranking Shodan's from Isshinryu were present. I saw many people that I used to train with; Sensei Gnome, Sensei Billow and many others, in addition to people that I knew from years of practicing martial arts. And then, there he was... as big as life, Mr. Johnson! What an amazing man! He brought one of his students from Iowa to help him demonstrate techniques. After dressing with all the high-ranking dons, we went into the dojo where Mr. Johnson greeted us and we bow in together. When entering or leaving a dojo you must bow; it is a form of respect and a way of greeting everybody. Everything that I had heard about Mr. Johnson was an understatement. He had an infectious smile and was humble over his good-natured brutality. I wanted to ask for his autograph, but I didn't because I believe that nobody is above us and nobody is below us. We are all equal, though some are more fortunate.

Mr. Johnson's brown-belt led us through calisthenics and other exercises. The high-ranking dons were upset that they couldn't grasp some of the techniques that he was demonstrating. In reality, his student was better than most of them. He also showed us a kata that used all eight stances; it was one that Mr. Johnson put together. None of us could do the kata, except Sensei Blate's group and Sensei Cotton's dojo who had already been taught the kata. Everyone seemed frustrated that a brown-belt was showing techniques, to icons in Isshinryu (with some currently in the Isshinryu hall of fame). I wanted to throw my belt away and put a white one on.

Mr. Johnson used Sensei Cotton as his uke and tossed him around hard. Wow, this was great! I never saw Sensei get punched, kicked or get up off the floor. I was in seventh-heaven watching Sensei get beat on. Mr. Johnson used an exercise from basics called shuto uch or basics number thirteen. Sensei Cotton threw a punch at Mr. Johnson and he was airborne, chest-high and parallel with the floor. He hit flat like a book and was on his feet for more. Sensei Cotton was tough as nails. He didn't get to be sensei by not being able to endure pain. I have watched sensei get beaten up by several people over the years only to see him come back to inflict vengeance on all those poor souls. I was proud to train with him because of his tenacity. It was an exciting night. If your technique isn't working, then go back to kata and bring it out of kata as you were taught. In reality, practicing a martial art is knowingly practicing something that you may never use in life. I derive great pleasure from practicing kata because I can work out anywhere. I don't need any equipment or another person as required in judo and aikido. The world is my dojo.

# The Isshinryuist: A Tale of Endurance

I attended another seminar with Mr. Johnson. He took one step forward and put up two blocks using his arms as if he were doing Sanchin kata and that was exactly what it was, the first step in Sanchin kata. We spent eight hours working on bunkai derived from that one move. It was hard to believe that anyone could do eight hours of bunkai from one move.

Mr. Johnson sponsored a week-long seminar at his dojo in Carson, Iowa where martial artists came to train. This included people who practiced different styles of karate. They flew in from different countries to learn the principles of Isshinryu. He ended one seminar (hearsay) using Sensei Blate as his uke. He told everyone in attendance that most altercations will end with a number five (lower block) or a number six (middle block) followed by a punch. These moves are taught as basics for beginners. Sensei Blate threw a punch at Mr. Johnson's chest. He blocked it and punched him in the chest. The people in attendance said that, "Sensei Blate turned three different colors and settled on blue, expelling every bit of air that was in him. Later, he sported a bruise on his entire back. When I saw Mr. Johnson crack a beer tab, I knew it was time to go home. Before leaving, I saw some guy flying in the air, four feet backwards before landing on his feet. I wasn't sure how wild he was once he started drinking.

Mr. Johnson is the person that I credit for taking the time to understand the intricacies of Isshinryu. I have a CD of Mr. Johnson (in Prada, IL) that Sensei copied for me. Mr. Johnson does all the open hand-katas and Sanchin kata without a gi top, allowing us to watch the contractions of his diaphragm while breathing and giving us a better understanding of Sanchin. My favorite spot on the CD isn't about kata rather, it's about Mr. Johnson doing bunkai on Sensei Tripp who is a fourth don trained by Sensei Cotton because I have never seen anyone do a back flip from using such little movement.

# The Isshinryuist: A Tale of Endurance

Mr. Johnson used Sensei Tripp as his uke because he was young, fit and over 6'2' tall. Mr. Johnson rolled up his sleeve and asked him to stand close. From less than two inches away, Mr. Johnson dropped his elbow on his chest bone. Before this happened, fear was in his eyes. Mr. Johnson dropped the elbow on his sternum and he landed on his back and he did a back-roll to boot. I don't fault Sensei Tripp for being scared. Some of Mr. Johnson bunkai can be seen on U tube. I encourage the reader to watch some, or all of them. It takes coordination to move like that and his kicks are superior.

Mr. Johnson was stationed in Okinawa while being in the Marines. He met Shimabuku there and started training with him. At that time, Shimabuku did not speak much English, if any. To train the marines, he broke down movements from kata into fifteen upper-body basics and eight kicks. It was an easier way to start teaching kata. When visiting an Isshinryu school you will notice that these basics are still the core of teaching a beginner. Mr. Johnson recalled that the dojo was directly in the sun's path making the cement hot. To solve this problem, they gathered a bucket of water and threw it on the cement to cool it down and allowing him to train. Many martial artists think that after decades of training they have enough knowledge to start changing   Isshinryu. I remember as if it were yesterday with Mr. Johnson saying, "If something isn't broke, then don't change it and Isshinryu works."

# The Isshinryuist: A Tale of Endurance

I don't add anything to the style I teach. I may show a different application or my understanding of how the technique works. The role of a martial artist is to pass down the methods, pure as possible. Isshinryu is going to be around until the end of time. I like to call Isshinryu by its nickname, "Basement Karate" because it takes place in almost every town. It isn't the most popular or glamorous karate out there, due to TV which portrays karate with high-kicks and leaps. Kicks and leaps violate two of the eight Isshinryu principles, "The body must change direction at any time and unbalance is unwanted weight."

When traveling to Michigan to check on my homes, I make a point to train with Sensei Snipe, he is Cotton's number one student; we are good friends and we have trained together for over twenty years. Snipes, represents the qualities of what I consider to be a good sensei. He will spend as much time as needed allowing the student to understand the moves in kata and break them out to work bunkai. We don't always agree on the move or who is correct, but we probe deeper for the answer. We try to incorporate the correct move is so we can pass down kata as taught by Tatsuto Shimabuku (Founder of Isshinryu).

Sargent

I attended a seminar that Mr. Johnson was teaching with Sensei Sargent. It was a fundraiser for Sensei Dodge who recently passed away and the proceeds were for his widow. Dodge was a student that trained with Shimabuku, along with Mr. Johnson and Sensei Ford. Sensei Sargent was a Marine drill sergeant that retired from the military and had one of the most booming voices I've ever heard. We were split into two groups; one with Sargent, who was teaching the historical aspect of Isshinryu and the other with Mr. Johnson who was teaching bunkai.

One of the stories that Sensei Sargent told us was when he was hired by the San Diego Chargers to teach the linesman body mechanics. He worked with a Pro-Bowler and the first thing the Pro-Bowler said was, "If you hurt me, I am going to sue." Sargent didn't believe in ki (energy flow). He believed that everything was related to body mechanics. Over the years, I have seen too many things to agree with him. He knew a lot about the history of Isshinryu and I was impressed with his stories. He used weapons a great deal, along with cane fighting which isn't part of the Isshinryu system. He provided a lot of information on his website making it worthwhile to visit. Sensei Sargent studied other styles and he sincerely believed that we don't need all of those katas. He said, "One kata will teach you the same thing." Again, I disagree. There are too many techniques to be learned from the Isshinryu system by doing kata. You may be able to do the technique, but the real test is: can you do it with positioning, placement and power. Each kata teaches you something different.

# The Isshinryuist: A Tale of Endurance

There is a move that comes out of SU NU SU, the only kata created by Shimabuku. It has a double punch delivered to the chin and solar plexus at the same time. I struggled for years to use this technique, but I only produced a powder-puff of the technique. Finally, I feel that I am able to strike with enough force to disable an opponent with this technique, but it took years. The nice thing about this technique is that if I change the timing in which the hands strike, it makes all the difference while creating an obstacle for the mind trying to defend the body.

During the seminar Sensei Sargent asked Sensei Bufford to be his uke. One of the techniques that he was going to demonstrate was from another style of martial arts. He wanted Sensei Bufford to strike him in the head using both of his open hands. At first Bufford was reluctant to hit Sargent and swung haphazardly at his head. Each time he tried, he struck Bufford in the head with his open hand while blocking him effortlessly. Sensei Sargent had one hand held up like a cobra with the other hand held under his elbow and was continuously making a circle like a cobra ready to lash out at Bufford's head. The entire group laughed as they watched Sensei Bufford's hair fly in the air, each time he struck his head. I stood next to Sensei Cotton, who seemed to enjoy this more than anyone in the group. Again, he struck him and his hair flew in the air. Sensei Bufford took off the kid gloves because he was totally frustrated. He was an accomplished martial artist with decades of training under his belt. He struck faster and harder, but ended up with the same results again and again, in spite of all his efforts, except now he heard continuous laughter, which felt like another slap in the face. After the demonstration Sensei Sargent bowed out and Sensei Bufford returned the bow. Sensei Cotton and I were still laughing and Sensei Bufford ended up being a good sport.

The next thing Sensei Sargent taught us was about distance. He asked if anyone in the crowd was good at head kicks. He had this student kick him in the head and every time he tried, he kicked him in the groin. This technique is nothing more than distance. That is why Sensei Sargent was beating him to the kick. "It's merely a distance thing," he said.

## Lodge

I designed and built a home in Northern Michigan. I was working on it every weekend, usually three-day weekends and nine hours each day. I called it "The Lodge." The first thing you do when buying land is to plant trees. I purchased fifteen trees, some with extremely large roots. The tree farm used heavy equipment to put them in my truck. When I tried to unload them, I wasn't able to move them around by myself. A neighbor, Big Jim, helped me, though I was reluctant to have him help because he recently, had open heart surgery. Big Jim almost hit his head while walking through the garage door, which was nearly seven feet tall. Jim seemed to be looking for a friend...and he found one. He had every tool imaginable and wanted to help anyone as long as he had someone to talk to. He struggled and panted while pulling the tree, which had me thinking that he was going to have another heart attack. I didn't want that to happen or I wouldn't be able to get the trees planted. He found out that he had bitten off more than he can chew and let go of the tree. A branch hit me in the eye making this my third black eye of the year. He apologized for letting go of the tree.

# The Isshinryuist: A Tale of Endurance

I was an administrator and felt they were going to fire me because of my black eyes. Luckily, this black eye was nothing like the one I received while playing racquetball. My cheekbone was so swollen that I could see it by looking normally out of my eye. My partner wanted to rush me to the hospital. I refused the offer and we finished the game. The eye hurt without even touching it. Being a martial artist one learns that after an injury, one does not touch or bump the injured area and it usually won't hurt. My other black eye occurred at the dojo. Anybody that has known me for very long can testify that I have had my share of pain. I wasn't aware yet that this would be a bumper year for pain. The Lodge was the biggest lone endeavor that I had ever undertaken physically and harder than I ever imagined.

I decided to build my house as soon as possible and I drew the plans on a large piece of card board. I took it to the township and they approved it and accepted my check. I was happy that I didn't have to pay an architect. My plan was to work three days a week on it, nine hours each day. This would allow me to have a life and keep up with my Isshinryu training, which was important. And for the next three years this is what I did. I hired as few people as possible to help me build the house.

I took all my tools up north. Once the truck was loaded, I threw in the saw-horses, but one hung out. "It's heavy and it won't fall out, I thought. On the way up north, I passed a gravel-hauling truck. As soon as I passed it, the saw horse fell out of the truck and onto the expressway. The driver swerved and went onto the shoulder and cut the wheel back causing the gravel truck to almost flip over. There was another gravel truck in front of me, and I imagined they were related because he tried to run me off the road.

# The Isshinryuist: A Tale of Endurance

Now I was on my way to building my dream home, the beginning of the Frenette Dynasty. Working long weekends made my job at the office more appealing and I was eager to get back to work. Another obstacle to building the house was distance. The "Lodge" was four hours away, eight hours round trip. In hind sight, I should have taken logistics into consideration before buying the land, but it sure is a beautiful piece of land.

I was excited that the lower deck was completed and I was building the back wall facing the Big Sable River. I took two weeks off without knowing what life had in store for me next, because if I did, I would have started crying and screaming for my mom. I ordered my windows and doors from the Home Depot near my house in Clarkston. I was under the impression that they would deliver them to Ludington. Instead, they dropped them off at my garage four hours away. This meant that I would have to transport them myself.

# The Isshinryuist: A Tale of Endurance

When I got home from work I needed to mow the lawn, grab my clothes and load the windows in my truck. As I was loading the windows, I realized I needed a knife to cut the rope, but I couldn't find one anywhere. This is when I remembered I had a Rambo knife. I have owned this knife for over ten years but have never even used it. "It was one nasty looking knife," I thought. It was green and black with a blade about five inches long with serrated edges. I got the knife and began moving quickly trying to get an early start. I laid the knife on the tailgate. As I finished loading and tying down the windows, I jumped up on the tailgate. It was the beginning and the end of my two week vacation. I must've stepped on the back of the Rambo knife allowing the point to pop-up a little bit. When I swung my right foot up on to the tailgate, the knife went through my tennis shoe severing a major artery. Let the festivities begin! I grimaced, but never yelped, though it did hurt. When I looked down at my foot there was blood gushing out of the top part of my shoe and pulsating out of the shoe lace holes. They say that you never know if you will go into shock upon seeing your own blood, and I was about to see almost every bit of blood I owned. I was calm through the entire incident. I yelled for my neighbor, whose door was more than three-hundred and fifty feet away, but there was no response. I bent over and squeezed my foot to keep it from bleeding. I walked over to his house being bent over and going up a small steep hill. As I knocked on his door there was a puddle of blood accumulating. Joe took one look at me and told me to get in his truck. I insisted on taking mine because I didn't want to get blood all over his truck. I started walking down the hill and bent over, holding my foot. Joe ran by me. I retrieved a five gallon bucket to submerge my foot in, which didn't work entirely because some blood got in the truck. Joe and I headed to the hospital. We discussed going to a Care Clinic, which was closer, but decided on the Osteopathic Hospital in Pontiac. We made the right choice...

# The Isshinryuist: A Tale of Endurance

The hospital was at least fifteen minutes away. I was holding my foot to keep the blood from flowing; the bucket held a lot of blood. Joe pulled up to the Emergency Entrance. Five employees were just standing around smoking and talking. When they saw me get out of the truck with blood gushing out of my foot, they dropped their cigarettes and started running towards me. The last thing I said to Joe was, "Don't let my windows get stolen." They put me in a wheelchair and ran through the triage area and into an ER room where there were five people waiting for me. They tossed me on a stretcher and a doctor grabbed my foot and squeezed the laceration while a nurse inserted an IV and another nurse connected some type of blood or plasma to it. I remember how the IV nurse was frantically stabbing something in my arm. I looked at his badge...his name was Chuck. I yelled, "Chuck, what the fuck are you doing?" Afterwards, I passed out for a few minutes. When I woke up, they informed me that I had flat-lined and lost four pints of blood. At this point I talked to everyone and tried to make the doctor laugh who was holding the wound closed. They asked me if I was in the military or with the Special Forces. My answer was, "No." However, it impressed me that they would think so. I attributed my survival to my Isshinryu and endurance training. I was stable and waiting for a vascular surgeon. The doctor continued to squeeze my foot until they took me into surgery. He squeezed so hard and for so long that it was really getting sore. They asked, "Have you eaten anything?" I mentioned a pork chop left over from yesterday's dinner. The anesthetist said, "That I would need a spinal." I told him that I didn't want one. They mentioned that they would probably have to amputate my leg unless I got a spinal. I looked at the doctor who was holding my foot for guidance; we started to bond after hours of looking at each other. He nodded at me and I replied, "Since, you put it that way, the spinal doesn't sound that bad." I leaned forward giving them access to my lower spine. The doctor and I headed to surgery. After that, I don't remember a thing. I didn't feel pain because of all the drugs. They pumped so many fluids in me that when I looked in the mirror my ears looked fat.

I called a couple of people to let them know I wouldn't be going up North to build the house. I also called my friend, Terrence, but I still can't remember making these calls. Now, the matter at hand is that I had to pee and I couldn't. I tried to use the plastic jug, the one that hangs off the side of the bed, but no luck. I couldn't walk because of the spinal and I made every effort to wiggle a toe, unsuccessfully. This "no pee issue" was becoming a problem, so I hit the call button and waited for someone to respond. I explained to the nurse that if she helped me to the bathroom, I would be able to pee. Two nurses attempted to lift me by holding me under both arms, but my weight was too much for them and they set me back on the bed. I tried using the plastic jug again, but nothing. No one in their right mind asks for a catheter to be shoved up their penis. But at that point I pleaded with the nurse to relieve my bladder. When the nurse left to grab the catheter kit, I grabbed the plastic jug again and started to think of a waterfall. I was imagining the water splashing over the ledge and hitting the steps, making a lot of spray. It worked and it took some pressure off my bladder. The nurse showed up with the tube, which was no longer needed. Most people wouldn't recognize me because my head was so swollen from the IVs. Reality was starting to sink in as I climbed "Maslow's Hierarchy of Needs." How was I going to build the Lodge? What was going to happen with my Isshinryu career? The doctor came into the room holding my chart. He told me that I was being released this morning. What the fuck, I couldn't even walk.

# The Isshinryuist: A Tale of Endurance

While building the lodge I met a new woman who was wealthy and a know-it-all. She didn't work, which gave her time to read four newspapers daily. We dated for about six months. Her kids were snobs and the daughter asked me, "People actually think you're funny." Her daughter drove a Jaguar to high school while her son was given a position at his father's company making 80k right out of high school. I called the rich girl to see if she would pick me up and she agreed. I started to get the feeling back in my legs once they started rolling me down the hallway. They gave me a set of crutches as a good bye present.

When I got home, the rich girl took good care of me. Her daughter graduated from high school that same evening. I thought with the Vicodin and the crutches, I would be able to attend. The graduation took place at the Pistons Stadium in Auburn Hills. It felt as if the stadium was ten miles away from the car. When I made it to the line, the attendants took one look at me and summoned an elevator (pain has its privileges). I used the crutches to get to my seat. Everyone had shoes on and it was crowded. I was guarding my foot; it was all I cared about.

I was supposed to meet the rich girl for dinner at an expensive restaurant the next day, but I wanted to take care of my foot. The pain medicine wasn't working. I got a six pack of beer to ease the pain along with the Vicodin. The phone rang and rang, and I knew it was the rich girl, but I didn't respond because I was having a good time now that the pain was gone, thanks to the cocktails. The rich girl showed up after dinner and was ready to chew me out. After taking one look at me she decided it made no sense to argue with a fool. After she left, I finished the last beer and got ready to crutch my way to bed. I hit my little toe (of my injured foot) on a bi-fold and I was amazed it didn't hurt. I had broken my little toe-I just didn't know it yet. The cut and the broken toe worked in unison producing more pain.

My boss called me the following day because Terrence had told her what happened. I asked if I could cancel my vacation and come back as soon as I was ready, she agreed. I returned to work on crutches. I used the stairs, but these were not your usual stairs. It was a one-hundred-year-old building. When the kids ran through the halls and came up against these battleship-gray stairs, they immediately, stopped. The stair tread was no wider than eight-inches. As soon as I sat in my chair, I passed out and slept for a short period. Later, I went to the administrative office to greet everyone and to hear them make a big fuss over my foot. To prevent infection, I cleaned and wrapped my foot twice a day. In spite of this, it looked like it was ready to split open and everyone that saw it agreed. The surgeon had made an incision about four inches long and he put in eight stitches. The cut was completely red, and where there were no stitches holding it together, it was spreading as much as a half inch. I was concerned about my house and the rain the structure was taking. I called Ed, a carpenter who was working with me. I asked if he could put some Thompson's Water Seal over the flooring. He said that he would, but it didn't get done. Ed was a heavy drinker. The last time I talked to Ed he was in jail for drunk driving. They let him out early due to overcrowding. Unfortunately, he was still drinking.

When I saw the vascular surgeon he felt for blood flow in my foot and told me that everything was working fine and that he was pleased. When I returned to the dojo I wore socks and shoes and did light workouts. Later on when I shed my shoes it felt as if I was walking on a finger and my balance was off while doing katas. It took years to get my balance back and I credit kata in helping me make a full recovery.

# The Isshinryuist: A Tale of Endurance

I had to break it off with the rich girl and find a woman up North, one who lived near the lodge. I told her that I wouldn't be able to accompany her to California for Thanksgiving." While I was watching TV after working out with sensei, the rich lady showed up and I was caught dead in her head lights. She stormed in the house yelling at me while grabbing her belongings. I didn't say anything. I just took the ass-whipping. I knew that the less I said the better. I noticed that she left her car running, meaning this episode would be short-lived. She went into the bedroom and ripped up all the love letters she wrote and scattered them on the floor. Then she grabbed a water pitcher from the fridge and emptied it all over the kitchen floor (it was a good thing that the jug wasn't full). She broke my lighthouse from Maine by launching it across the room. She uttered a few choice words and then she left. Her best move was when she threw push-pins across the room and they shattered against the wall. I stepped on one, which produced a yelp, some blood and a hobble, but at least she never saw it.

When I got to work I showed Terrence, the breakup pictures. I told him that when you go through a break up, you should keep your head moving because it reduces the chances of getting your nose broken. A few weeks later, Terrence and his gal broke up. When she came over his house to return his belongings, she noticed that he kept wiggling his head. She asked, "What the fuck are you doing?" He told her, "Frenette said that I should keep moving my head, so when you strike me, you won't be able to break my nose." I got a belly laugh because I thought he knew that I was kidding.

# The Isshinryuist: A Tale of Endurance

Homeless Shelter

A security company wanted my business and made several trips to the front desk, inquiring whether I was at work. The employees told me that they didn't know what I was up to because, "...two big men keep looking for you." Mr. Jamal and Mr. Thomas were former cops that worked on the drug detail and were avid weight lifters. I became friends with Mr. Jamal, who took weight-lifting to another level. He did bench presses using 225 pounds, doing sets of twelve, twenty times. We met at my office to discuss business and ended up sharing information about the life path we had chosen. He shared stories about breaking into drug houses. He said, "He'd hit the first person that he saw and then run through the house hitting everyone until they were all subdued.

I worked with Mr. Jamal showing him some intricacies related to Isshinryu. He couldn't understand "the rub" technique and what I could do to him by applying it. He remarked, "Frenette...you are the only who has actually hurt me." I extended an invitation to him to meet Sensei Cotton, but he declined. I often listened to people's stories about how tough they are, to which I simply asserted: "Why don't you come to the dojo? I am sure sensei would love to have you visit." Everyone emphatically turned down my offer.

# The Isshinryuist: A Tale of Endurance

I worked at the homeless shelter for nearly a decade. It seemed as though everyone wanted to get up and tell their story. I had a friend who was an alcoholic, now an ex-alcoholic. He went to AA for twenty years, four times a week for two hours. Wouldn't a person be better off if they stayed away from an environment where they relive their story over and over again? There is a time to stand on your own two feet and quit relying on a crutch, especially if you're a martial artist; I hold all martial artists to a higher standard. A sensei is supposed to be an inspiration to his students. Isshinryu is a cloud which can never be grasped; the more one tries to seize it, the more the cloud disappears. There were times when I will visit a dojo and nobody will come over to talk to me, not even a hello. This is not how we greet people who come into a dojo. Other times, I am greeted with open arms and I am asked to do a kata or a bunkai demonstration. I perform with enough power to show students these are credible techniques, one that they may want to add to their repertoire of techniques. My goal is to be invited back as a friend and a teacher (sensei).

### Terrence

I admire my friend Terrence because of his determination in his workouts. I replicate his work ethic; he is a true professional. When I write memos or resumes, I envision Terrence standing over me with a ruler though he'd rather me think of him standing over me with a bat, instead. I met him while working at a homeless shelter. He was a thin, muscular man with a contagious smile and the whitest teeth you will ever see. His dress was impeccable down to his shoes. He dressed as though he were modeling for the Gentleman's Quarterly (GQ) magazine. In fact, you would think he was gay by his appearance. And the first time I met him, I asked, "Are you gay?" With a perplexed look on his face, he answered, "No!"

Terrence wore glasses most of his life, until he had Lasik surgery. He broke his glasses at the age of eight and his parents refused to buy him a new pair. Instead, he had to collect bottles until he gathered enough money to purchase a new pair. In the meantime, his parents didn't care if his school work suffered. This is how kids are made responsible and Terrence is one of the most responsible people I know.

Terrence was fit as a fiddle. While we were in my office I told him that I could knock the wind out of him by punching him through one of those thick, urban phone books. He said, "That is impossible." I showed him how to hold it up to his ribs and how to get in a stance. I threw a seiken (lunge punch) which set him back a little and then I threw a reverse punch using some ki and proper breathing. The air rifled out of him afterwards, he has never let me hurt him again.

We played tennis together a few times, but it didn't take long before his mindset shifted and focused on chasing women because he was recently divorced. It was funny to see his legs looking like two broom sticks coming out of his tennis shoes. I called him peg-leg, but not anymore; he recently finished a marathon and was turning his efforts towards becoming an ultra-marathoner (50 miles or longer). And to top it off, he was planning to do simulated Buds (Navy Seal) training. He built his legs up and they looked normal now.

Terrence and I went to a bar in Detroit. I was very careful about drinking and driving, especially with it being an hour's drive home. Here, I saw a different side of Terrence that I wasn't used to. He bothered two men so much that they jumped off their bar stools and were ready to confront him. I apologized for my friend's drunkenness, adding that he hadn't eaten since this morning. This explanation wasn't good enough for them as they were still headed our way. At this point, I told them in a stern voice, "If you go after him, I am involved!" They decided to go back to their seats. Prior to leaving, they went to the restroom, a place where my worst fear is to get stuck in the kidney with a knife while my back is turned. I was happy to leave. I offered to drive Terrence home, but he refused. I was amazed to watch him drive away showing no concern of ending up in jail.

# The Isshinryuist: A Tale of Endurance

On Monday, I noticed his demeanor was different; he looked scared. It took some prying to find out what was wrong. I persisted because I knew he probably did something dumb and whatever it was it was going to be good. He was at a wine-tasting party with his new gal, Susan. It was late when they left the party. Susan was exhausted and quickly fell asleep. After falling into a deep slumber, the new Ford Explorer was sliding across the road on its roof. (I bet Susan was thinking it was bad dream). The metal roof was shooting sparks as seen in action movies. When the vehicle came to a complete stop, they were both hanging upside down by their seat belts staring at each other. This was Terrence's version: He saw a dog cross his path and swerved to miss the dog. Here is what really happened: Terrence fell asleep at the wheel and woke up seeing a 25 foot metal light. He reacted by swerving over the curb and jerked the steering wheel back, which caused it to flip over. Terrence was faced with the dilemma of either calling his mother or the police. I would have chosen to call the police. When his mother arrived to pick them up, Susan met her future mother-in-law for the first time and said, "Hi, Mrs. Gilson. It's nice to meet you!" Ha! What a Kodak moment!

When he came to Northern Michigan to stay at the Lodge, we worked out together. He loved my house and was impressed that I had the fortitude to build such a home by myself. The neighborhood referred to me as "the man that actually built it by himself." Others in the neighborhood started to building houses, but gave up.

# The Isshinryuist: A Tale of Endurance

I took Terrence swimming at one of my favorite watering holes close to my house. The bridge railing had a drop of seventeen feet to the water. I have been on countless rides at amusement parks and most rides make me yawn. This bridge jump was different and the water moved at a fast pace. I showed Terrence where to stand before jumping in the ice cold river. I mentioned that this was the deepest part of the river, where he would miss the rocks. His eyes widen at the thought of jumping. A white truck pulled up and a heavy-set guy came running out of his truck and told Terrence, "He wanted to see me jump to my death!" I plunged into the water, but the frigid water was my last concern. It's landing on the rocks and hitting the water properly was my main concern. I jumped a few more times, but Terrence wanted no part of it.

I met Terrence for a summer camping excursion at the Manistee National Park in Michigan. He said that his main objective while he was driving northward was not to let Frenette hurt him. I asked him to bring the stick that I made for him, which isn't a bo until I taught him how to use it. He was overwhelmed at how hard it was to coordinate the moves. The moves we worked on for just a few short moments will take years of practice to master. Our friendship picked up right where it left off. He told me that he didn't eat meat anymore. While at the grocery store I tried to coax him into eating fried chicken. "Come on! You're black; it's a staple of your culture." Still, he did not budge. Later, I started thinking about eliminating meat from my own diet. I made the decision, and have not eaten meat since.

# The Isshinryuist: A Tale of Endurance

My son knows me as carnivorous Lar and thought this phase will be short-lived, but he soon realized that I was serious and I have identified some areas that will promote excellent health and decrease the chances of me becoming a burden to my children in old age. Most people die prematurely because of the poor choices they make, smoking is one of them. More people die in America from overeating than from not having enough to eat. My thoughts towards longevity are as follows: one 81 milligram aspirin a day, one citrus fruit daily and a daily strenuous one-hour workout. I will not delve into this subject in depth, but provide the principles only. Personally, I follow the Mediterranean Diet.

Terrence and I went for a bike ride on the gravel roads and he was game for anything. I left him behind in a trail of fine dust. I waited for him thinking he may get lost. When he saw me, he yelled, "You don't have to wait for me, I am just catching up." In reality, he was so, so far behind that I literally had enough time to get off of my bike and work on my katas.

Terrence reminded me of the Monty Python character who had his arm cut off during a sword fight; then his other limbs are cut off one by one until there is nothing left, but his torso. And he still wouldn't give up and wanted a sword put in his mouth to continue fighting. Before we ended the bike ride, I told Terrence that I would ride on the road's shoulder. So if a car hit me, we knew that the driver hated everybody, but if they hit only him, this would be a good indicator of it being racially motivated. Terrence, among others, didn't always appreciate my sense of humor.

Asheville

I was at the Wedge Brewery in Asheville with my friend Sammy enjoying the libations of the Wedge, along with the free shelled peanuts, which served as dinner sometimes. On this particular night we met Rusty John. He wasn't real tall, but he was wide and looked even wider wearing a black leather coat. It was near closing time when Rusty found out that I practiced martial arts. He wanted to show me a technique he had used to subdue many assailants. The next thing I know, we knocked over three bar stools; the bartender was angry and asked us to quit. Rusty actually had me there for a moment. This happened for two reasons. I didn't know he was going to do it and two I had been drinking. Afterwards, I thought that maybe he was pretty good or I was losing it. Rusty grabbed a growler (64 ounces) of Iron Rail and asked us to come to his house where we could exchange some techniques. Sammy and I jumped in his car and headed to Rusty's house. We ended up in his backyard. It was a country setting in the mountains with lots of fallen leaves. What convinced us to go to Rusty's is that he mentioned that he has some kick-ass weed. After smoking some and taking a swig of some of the Iron Rail, Rusty was in form and ready to show me his fighting techniques. On every move I snuffed him and in some cases I hit him four times before he reacted. At one point he was actually fighting and I was just playing. We worked on technique for a couple of hours and when we wanted to smoke some weed, we could not find it. Rusty blamed Sammy for his loss, and talking to Sammy was like talking to a fool because he finished off that growler by himself. Rusty made a comment that I had to agree with, I always know where I put my weed. I was convinced that Sammy stole it and I had to apologize to him later when Rusty found it.

# The Isshinryuist: A Tale of Endurance

It was Thanksgiving Eve and Rusty had to drive to Battle Creek, Michigan for Thanksgiving. Later, his friends told me that he was upset for me putting bruises all over him and that his soreness lasted for weeks. I believe that the reason I was able to dissect Rusty's techniques was my diligence to train and knuckle-conditioning; they hurt even when I'm playing. Rusty never exchanged techniques with me again, though he spoke highly of my Isshinryu skills. Shortly after this, I talked to Rusty's wife and she said that he mentioned that I was really good. I professed that I was not, but that I knew people who were. I guess that is one of the reasons I train. What Mr. Johnson has done with Isshinryu stays in my head and my heart. My wife says that I talk of Mr. Johnson often and she wonders how many times his name is mentioned around the world in a day. I had spent many years trying to emulate Sensei Benson, but very few people can because he was like the Bruce Jenner of martial arts before he became Catlin.

# The Isshinryuist: A Tale of Endurance

There were a few incidents at the Wedge that happened when the libations flowed freely. We were all out there having a good time, when a man seemed to come out of nowhere. He started talking with us while we were on the porch of the bar. When I returned from getting peanuts and beer, I heard them talking about martial arts and mentioning my name. This guy started telling me about how he kicked seventeen peoples' butts last year and that he wanted to train with me. He wasn't drinking, but he sure was acting goofy. He was behaving like Shaolin Tiger or someone from one of those Chinese martial arts movies. I got tired of his rhetoric and told him to get, the fuck away from me. Just before I told him this, the crowd disappeared and went indoors and we were the only ones left. Unexpectedly, he threw a haymaker (sucker punch) when I wasn't ready, trying to take my head-off. I was thinking that if I had touched his chin and turned his head, it would nullify his power. And that was my intention, but Mitzi Gami had other ideas; she had me parry with him (match distance) and at the same time I hit him with two palm heels, about a half inch above the nipples, making him go airborne, but not very high. He went about eight feet in distance and I thought he was going to hit his head on the scrap metal artwork that was welded in the shape of a table. Then the rubber from his tennis shoes grabbed the cement, he hit hard. It took the fight out of him. I was kind and I didn't take the boots to him. Afterwards, he was on all fours trying to get on his feet while looking up at me like I was Superman. I saw myself in a different light and I thought, "Dweeb, you did that?" Immediately, I uttered some kind words to him: "Get the Fuck out of here!" I watched him limp away and disappear into the darkness. I went inside to say goodbye to my friends.

Later, I was hired as a property manager in St. Croix, the US Virgin Islands. And there was a quite a prelude leading up to it. It seemed as though everything I touched in the past four years, financially that is, turned to crap. One of the things that I was fortunate for was the insight to save twenty percent of my wages creating a nest egg for hard times. I learned these principles from Isshinryu and that is how I managed my money. I waited for big announcements in the economy. Over the years I read several books on economics, including authors like Adams, Misner, Pierce, Keynes and others. I would slide money into risky accounts after hearing about big events and pulled it back in two days while clearing a substantial amount of money and securing it into a fixed interest account. I received a call from my account manager who told me that I would have to wait a full thirty days before I could shift money around and she took me to lunch to tell me this. I bought the most expensive item on the menu. Not long afterwards, I quit my job. During the Obama election I slide some more money over again, but I had to wait thirty days. Using thirty thousand, I made almost thirteen thousand dollars. I was concerned that I might lose most of it, but it worked and I haven't done it since.

Afterwards, I put as much money into education as I could. I started taking real estate classes to become a broker. The testing for obtaining this license were some of the hardest I have ever taken. I failed the first class, along with most people there, and signed up for another class. The classes had a ninety-five percent failure rate. I formed a study group with a girl who also failed the first class. We studied every week until the very last week. But first let's talk about Si and some others in the class. The man that taught the class was a real estate attorney. He gave his spiel about how hard the class was. He said he was concerned about passing the Broker's test when he took the test. The couple that sat behind me should have gotten a room because they were too old to be making out in class and they both failed. Then, there's was my friend with the red nose who looked like a major alcoholic who also failed because he was always texting. My favorite story is that of Si. Si was a successful real estate agent in Florida. He said, "This test can't be that hard." Si attended every class and paid attention. His cockiness started leaving him after each passing class. And as we entered the mid-point of the real estate course, he mentioned that he went to Barnes and Noble to study until closing time almost every night. During the first and second real estate class I walked a half-hour each way and studied two hours a day, seven days a week. A week before the test I asked my study partner if she was ready to meet? She said that she was going to the movies with her husband. I kept studying because I don't leave anything to chance. The day of the test I talked to Si and he told me his car was packed and he was ready to go to Florida. Afterwards, he was going to get his wife and come back to North Carolina and open a construction business and sell real estate with his wife. The test was given and it was timed at three hours. This was my third attempt at passing this test. You get the chance to take it over twice in each class and I failed it twice already. The class was four hours in length and we met two nights a week over four months, not to mention all the studying involved in order to pass. After the test, we waited outside in the mall hallway. Everyone was nervous wondering if they will pass, except for a few that worked in real estate offices. The instructor approached me with a folded paper and a look on his face that said, "I'm sorry, but you didn't make it." I immediately thought that I have one more try before I had to pay another $600. When I looked at the paper, I was delighted to find out I passed, but not by much; but passing is all that matters. I subscribe to the thought, "You know what they call the person in medical school with the lowest grade, Doctor!"

I spoke with Si, he told me he failed the test along with my study partner, he told me that he didn't think he could ever pass the test. My study partner said, "That she was not going to try again. The couple I mentioned earlier (that needed a room) did not pass, and my friend with the red nose, failed by one point...how disheartening.

I was proud that I passed and the next day I enrolled to take the real estate exam at the state level. The test was two weeks away and it cost another $100. I kept up my study habits as though I was still in class. I've never encountered a test with so many ambiguous questions. I had to take an oath that I wouldn't discuss the test with anyone or risk losing my license. To enter the building, two types of ID were required: a driver's license and a passport. A proctor was watching every move. It was another timed three hour test. The only thing allowed was a calculator and a scrap piece of paper that included your name, which had to be turned in afterwards. The test screen came up and read "Failed." I let out an f-bomb because I just couldn't believe it. The proctor told me not to worry because I was almost there. I went home and told my wife that I failed; she thought I was kidding until I registered for another class. I scheduled the test two weeks out and kept up my study habits until the day of the test. When I sat down this time, I made the sign of the cross like a good Catholic before I hit the "submit" button. It appeared on the screen as "<PASSED>" It was going to be a Wedge night!

I will never let this license lapse; it is honored in ten states. I talked to my wife about us becoming a husband and wife team. She replied, "Please don't ask me to go through all that studying. It gets better...I entered real estate in the second worst depression that the United States has ever seen. I sold one house and I haven't seen the money, it was on a two year contingency. This isn't a business, I am a servant. I disliked almost everything about it, but I give credit to all the people that can make it work.

# The Isshinryuist: A Tale of Endurance

In Asheville, I lived next to twelve clay tennis courts. There were some basketball hoops and two stripped tennis hard courts for practicing against a backboard with a line painted to simulate the top of the tennis net. It was a nice place to train. There was a gazebo on top of the hill, a place where the homeless, prostitutes and junkies hung out.

This is where I trained for the next four years. When I first started training everyone thought I was crazy. But after seeing me train every day, they gained respect for me with some complimenting me on my tenacity. The clubhouse workers told me they liked me being there because I kept a lot of the riffraff away.  After training, I would go down to the tennis courts to play doubles for two hours. I was definitely tired after the three and half hour workout.

The first time I walked on the courts to play tennis, I was asked what number I was. I told them that most people thought of me as a zero. They didn't really laugh. This is where I first met Ted Heady or Coach, a gruff speaking person whom I didn't care for at first, because he was so crabby. He let me play and I wasn't very good when I arrived in Asheville. Many people were told that they needed to take lessons to play with "these guys." I love tennis, but it was just another way for me train. The only reason Coach let me play was because of my ability to chase down balls. The tennis players at Aston Park were good and had been playing for decades. They could make a tennis ball sing a solo.

# The Isshinryuist: A Tale of Endurance

While I was working on my katas, a gentleman was rolling his wheelchair towards me. I asked, "Are you here for private lessons?" He laughed and answered, "No!" He was here to see if I would play tennis with his wife. He said, "That she was a good player. I agreed to play and I met her on the court. The temperature was pressing ninety degrees and it was close to noon. I saw her waiting for me. She was a small-framed lady who was short in stature and over seventy years of age. We started by volleying back and forth. I could tell from the way she was hitting, that she played often. During the match she took me to the far corners of the court. I didn't even get a game the first set. She hit the ball long, then short and there was nothing I could do to beat her. She yelled at me to get under the ball. She won the second set and wanted to play a third, but the heat took a toll on her. She had to deal with my conditioning and quit during the third set. I had fun and I was glad I was on the far court going unnoticed. The bonus with tennis and Isshinryu is that they're sports that you can play to life's end. When Walter Cronkite was on his death bed, I heard a quote of him saying, "I wish my legs had the strength to carry me for one more game of tennis." You may think this is a strange request and wonder why he didn't say that he wanted to make love to his wife one more time. When the tennis bug gets you, you are hooked. If someone were to ask me right now what I would like to do, the answer would be: "I would like to be on the tennis court playing tennis with my son."

# The Isshinryuist: A Tale of Endurance

I have been all over the United States by car, train, Greyhound Bus and plane. I have also been to Canada and Mexico many times. The worst mode of transportation by far is Greyhound. The only mode of transportation that it beats is walking and I am not totally sure of that. I took the Greyhound bus once, just for the experience and what an experience it was. They say that sometimes your worst experiences turn out to be your best. Well, it wasn't like that with Greyhound. When I moved to Asheville I had three vehicles and needed to leave one in Asheville, NC. The ride began in Asheville and my destination was Grand Rapids, Michigan, a ten and a half hour trip by car. The ride on the Greyhound Bus started off being two hours late. I got tired of asking when the bus was coming or whether it had left another bus depot.

I found out later that the sole fact someone was riding Greyhound meant they were down on their luck. I have driven lots of miles and people usually complimented me on what a good and trustworthy drive I am. The principle I use, don't let the other driver's problem become yours, or simply put, you give yourself enough distance between cars according to the road conditions.

I've been passed by a lot of Greyhound buses and noticed that they know how to drive. They use their signals while changing lanes and drive as though the bus is an extension of their body. I felt confident that we would arrive in one piece and in an acceptable time frame. There were hookers, gang-bangers and druggies, all riding side-by-side on the bus.

# The Isshinryuist: A Tale of Endurance

The bus arrived and we were excited to be on our way. We were in the mountains and the bus was passing everyone; the mountains were high and curvy and it was almost nightfall. The bus driver put on the dome lights, but it was not enough light to read by and they had a yellowish haze because of old lens covers. The bus was noisy. I sat next to a man who had a four hour phone conversation with the same person. I couldn't hold my pee any longer and I needed to use the bathroom, which was located in the rear of the bus. I was grateful the bus had one. I have been on buses that made stops for passengers to use the bathroom. As I stood up to walk to the restroom, I struggled getting to the back because the bus was shifting and mirroring the curves. When I opened the door and looked at the toilet, I was disgusted to see brown liquid close to the top. The toilet wasn't working and hadn't been flushed in quite some time. Not only that, it was sloshing back and forth and it was gaining momentum as I was about to urinate. There was nothing to hang on too. It was like being on a ship in a violent storm. That brown liquid was cresting and about to land on me. I was back as far as I could possibly get and it smelled, but that wasn't my concern. I definitely didn't want the brown liquid on me for the duration of the trip. I was so glad when the bathroom visit was over. Afterwards, I zigzagged back and forth to my seat unscathed. I was tired, but I didn't want to go to sleep because I wanted to see the facial expression of the next person attempting to use the restroom. It wasn't long before the young, black gentleman, who was sitting near me got up to use the restroom. After coming out of the bathroom, he complained that the bathroom should be shut down for the rest of trip. The bus started smelling to the point where people didn't even want to breathe. When we arrived at the station everyone stood up in hope of getting off the bus before the next person. Some were more adamant about it than others, as others raised their voices about the disgusting smell. At our next layover, the bus was late by five hours.

A female passenger found a bar within walking distance and got wasted, vomited and passed out on the sidewalk. She was comatose, lying up against the building. The group that I was mingling with was black and felt as though I should take care of her because she was white. I told them that she didn't look like a rookie and that the lord took care of fools and babies. I found out that our next bus wasn't coming until the morning. The dispatcher told me I could ride the bus to Nashville and that I would arrive at my final destination at the same time. I opted to go to Nashville, which was six hours out of the way, but at least I could sleep. The bus ride took me forty-two hours by the time I arrived home.

Jim Smith, Sensei's number one student was there. I liked working out with him because he didn't hurt me like sensei. We went through all our katas together and when I saw him doing something different, we stopped and discussed it, with Jim usually being right. If we didn't agree, we asked sensei, he had the correct answer. After he figured it out, he did bunkai on us. My first choice as always was for him to use Jim. This would be a spectator sport if it was left up to me. Jim was tough as nails.

I know a lot of people in Michigan because this is where my roots are and I have spent most of my life enduring the cold, wind and rain. The standing joke about Michigan weather is, "What do you call it after two days of rain, Monday." The rain is only interrupted for a moment and that's to rain harder. I lived in the Tri-City area, which encompasses Flint, Detroit and Ann Arbor and is noted for some of the cloudiest weather in the country.

I remember my past life as a rough carpenter, there were very few days that I went home thinking that it had been a really nice day outside. My relatives thought I was always picking on their state. They rarely went anywhere; if they traveled to northern Michigan they were excited and started talking about it weeks in advance. A majority of them have never lived more than fifteen miles from where they grew up. I enjoy gathering new input by going new places and meeting people from different cultures. The reason I ended up in Asheville goes back to an International Economics class. The professor talked about the building of the Biltmore Mansion. The instructor mentioned, before the mansion was built, the Vanderbilt's hired weather consultants to find the nicest weather in the country; this was before air conditioning. The weather consultants came up with Asheville, North Carolina. Asheville is like the melting pot of the world. Meeting people that had live in different countries and eager to share their views on American politics. This made me look at our country in a different light and it wasn't always positive.

# The Isshinryuist: A Tale of Endurance

Asheville has very few mosquitoes and mosquitoes were put on Earth to make us appreciate flies. I trained in Asheville for over three and half years and it would've never happened in Michigan, even with bug spray. The tourist industry for Michigan advertises "Go MI." I don't really want to pick on Michigan too much because it is pretty and I have had a lot of fun there. However, the biting insects in Michigan are bad and the only state to beat out Michigan is Maine. In Michigan the mosquitoes come out at dusk and the eager ones come out earlier. If you lay out on a lawn chair in the sun, the mosquitoes will come out of the grass where the lawn chair made some shade and attack your behind. The horseflies can fly circles around you while you're riding a bike. And not to mention the deerflies, ticks and the infamous black flies. The quote from Lewis and Clark Expedition was, "For the love of anthropology and mankind, we wouldn't go back into the woods because of the black flies." You can always tell a veteran Michigander because as soon as they get their first mosquito bite, they go indoors. They know the attacks will increase and it won't get better. In Maine there are hybrid horseflies that have the same qualities of an F17 fighter jet. When they land on your body, it is an immediate bite with blood coming out. They are known as Green Heads or Greenies and once you see one, you won't have to ask why they are called Greenies.

# The Isshinryuist: A Tale of Endurance

I was reunited with my wife after leaving the Virgin Islands. I started my training ritual near the twelve green clay tennis courts. This is where the crack-heads, the homeless and the lazy ones hang out under the gazebo which was about three hundred feet away from where I trained and up a small grassy hill. The gazebo was covered with a decorative roof that matched the clubhouse. It had a cement base with two picnic tables inside it. I liked doing pushups on the picnic tables in the gazebo because I don't have to worry about hitting my chin and I liked positioning my feet and hands on the four corners; it worked the chest muscles a little differently. I talked to everyone in the gazebo and some of the people that hung out there were interesting. Everybody seemed glad that I was back in Asheville where I had a good friendship base. I hung out with people whose ages spanned from their twenties to their eighties. For me, age isn't a factor in developing friendships.

I started playing tennis again with Lawyer Bob and the results were the same. I haven't picked up a tennis racquet in seven months. He was disappointed that he couldn't beat me after all his practice. I asked him to play doubles with us in the morning and he said, "Everyone is always telling me where to stand and how to play." I told Bob that they never say that to me when I play. He said, "You're a warrior; they leave you alone." I guess rank had its privileges. I was back to living off of my savings because my wife wasn't about to help me and she wouldn't even put me on her health insurance because it would be too expensive… There is something to be said about diet and exercise and a cheap wife. When I go to the doctor and fill out a new patient form, it seems to have three-hundred items listed, from diabetes to illnesses that I can't even pronounce. But I knew that if they were listed, it wasn't a good thing to have. I checked nothing and wrote in the blank space that I was allergic to pain; I thanked kata for my health.

# The Isshinryuist: A Tale of Endurance

There are a couple of ways to check to see if you are in decent condition: one is to lie on the floor and see how fast you could get up. And the one I use daily to monitor my well-being. I never use my hands to assist me while getting out of a chair, ever. I know if this started happening, it was time to start taking measurements for my coffin.

Asheville is an exciting place. There is a group for everyone in Asheville. If a person was into something weird, I am sure there would be a group for it in Asheville. It was such a fun place to live that I wasn't getting out the resumes that I should to find a job. Finally, a job offer came through, but did not pay a lot of money. The southern states don't pay as much as the Midwest, but I accepted it. This was the first company I worked for where people were actually happy to be there. We agreed on the rate, but my new boss chiseled a thousand dollars off my annual pay on the day I was about to start, but I agreed because I needed some income. My new boss was from Chile and so was my wife; it seemed as though I was surrounded by Chileans. I was given my own personal golf cart. This was a beautiful resort with a lake and lot of amenities. It was half hour away from my home. I thought they would give me a truck for on-call. My boss told me he would email me my schedule. They wanted me to work double-shifts and be on-call 24/7, and to top it off he wanted me to work a ten-hour shift and nothing was ever mentioned about this during the hiring process. I disregarded working the ten hours and worked eight hours only.

# The Isshinryuist: A Tale of Endurance

It was fun to drive the golf cart around the resort. On the fourth day he wanted me to help someone put a towel box together by the pool when my eight hour shift was up. I told the Chilean that I was going home. He told me he had put me down for ten hours and I was telling him that I hired in for eight. He called me back and wanted me to stop and see him. I stopped by his office and he told me that I was salaried and he explained that he worked long hours. He also indicated that my excel sheet showed that I must work ten hours. I told him that it was an excel sheet and that he could have written twelve hours. He said that twelve hours was too long of a shift. And I told him that ten was too long for me. I gave him back his phone, keys and left. When it's time to stand up, do so! Don't let people take advantage of you. If I worked ten hours, along with the on-call, I would be too tired to train. Now I was back to training, tennis and catching a good movie because I was exhausted from all that exercise.

I trained in Isshinryu for an hour and fifteen minutes which was an arduous workout in itself and then I played tennis for two hours. On the tennis courts they called me the runner because I loved to run balls down. On the other days, after my workout, Mike Sugarman and I would go for a pitcher of IPA and lunch. He was an interesting man who knew every rule in tennis and possessed a PhD. I taught him Bo kata, which is not how Isshinryu is taught, but he was paying me for private lessons and I brought him back into the realm of teaching him empty hands, which is usually taught first. The first thing he learned is that Isshinryu makes the smartest person feel dumb and I have never met anyone that did not feel the same way.

# The Isshinryuist: A Tale of Endurance

Mike brought me a hunk of Bamboo that was two and half inches in diameter. He was proud of this beast of a bo, but it was a little long and I asked him to cut it down to match his height and he did so for his next private lesson. A bo should be no taller than the karate-ka using it. He carried his bo in his truck and wasn't afraid to use it on someone, if he needed to. He told me there were a few times when he pulled it out of his SUV to get his way.

Mike was always fighting with someone, be it in person, on the internet or through the use of a lawyer and he would spend thousands of dollars to prove his point. He reminded me of Sensei Cotton where he created more enemies than he needed to. On the other hand, Mike had a kind heart and was an advocate for the poor, the homeless and anyone down on his luck.

Mike would take on a Governor, a Senator, and even the USTA tennis association. I think one of his regrets in life was that he didn't know about Isshinryu earlier. I believe he was one of those people that would have proved this theory wrong, "Many will enter through the doors of Isshinryu, but few will remain." Mike asked me, "Does your wife know how good you are in Isshinryu?" My reply: "She thinks I am the hardest working man she has ever met, but she could care less about my Isshinryu and she would have difficulty naming two of my empty hand katas." Since starting my training in Isshinryu in 1972, Isshinryu has always been on my mind and I have only taken a few months off. One of the teachings from Isshinryu that I follow is, "Fierce in battle, gentle in life." And I can honestly say that I probably wouldn't be around today if it weren't for Isshinryu.

AL

During my workouts I throw an average of 450 kicks. My son laughs at my legs because the hair doesn't grow on the calves because my gi rubs the hair off. As a martial artist I believe in cross training and lean more towards aerobics, but since arriving home from the Virgin Islands my thought has evolved to adding more strength training. I am doing more strength training for two reasons: 1) I want to put my katas on U Tube and they can always be better. 2) I had been in so many near altercations while living on the Virgin Islands that I think it wouldn't hurt to be stronger as well. The training routine that I am currently working on is doing kata for over an hour after work in the community room. This is the closest thing that I have ever had to my own dojo, besides the one in my basement. I also hit the fitness trail three times a week. My goal with the fitness trail is to do more than I did the last time I was there. I was running for an hour, three times a week, but dropped it because running doesn't give me the desired workout. Since implementing this new workout regime I have lost ten pounds and have considerably more strength. My worst area is doing chin-ups, and, really, how often do we use those muscles in real life?

My favorite person to play tennis with is known for his aliases as "The Bruiser," "Albo," "Boy," and my best friend. We began to play tennis twenty-two years ago on Sanibel Island. At that time we didn't know how to play tennis, so we made up our own rules and played it like any other game, the one who got to fifteen won. He is still my favorite person to play with, but I can't beat him anymore. There was a time when I used to beat him just like the rooster beat the dog with a stick in the cartoon "The Foghorns."

# The Isshinryuist: A Tale of Endurance

We have played "Opens" all over the country: the Boston Open, The Michigan Open, The San Diego Open, the New Hampshire Open and The Asheville Open, just to mention a few. An Open consists of the best of three sets and three sets are needed to win, but only one set can be acquired in a day to win the Open. It can be won in as short as three or in five days. Neither side is resting; this is athleticism at its best. This is where the saying, "You heard of "Big Dad. Now you have to face him" was born. When the boy lost, I told him, "You played well, boy, but I didn't play that well." This really drove the dagger home after beating him.

During the San Diego Open, Al was training with the Navy Seals on Coronado Island near San Diego and I came to town to visit him. He was in the best shape of his life. The Seals required that everyone must have breakfast together. They did a three mile run to the mess hall for breakfast and everyone had to be seated for chow at 6:00 A.M. He told me that the instructors could break anyone if they wanted to. A cadet would gladly ring the bell to quit the Seals. It's harder to make the Seals than it is to graduate from Harvard. They had chin-up bars all over the beach, and along with the sand and the ocean, they had everything they needed to break a young cadet. Al doesn't like lying on the beach because of the sand and his experience with it. He said they were made to do sit-ups in the ocean with everyone locking arms. He said, "I felt like I was going to drown when the waves pushed us under the ocean."

On the Discovery Channel, you can see the Seals carrying a boat on their head. One person broke his neck while carrying the boat during the time Al trained there. The instructors wanted to make a collegiate athlete quit. They used a bulldozer to make a hill of sand on the beach and made him run up and down the hill for hours until he quit.

Al said, "On the beach some of the applicants claimed they were dehydrated, which allowed them to go to the sick bay and take the easy life until they felt better." To sort out the liars, the instructors had something that looked like a turkey baster. They made the applicant drop his shorts and they stuck this in their rectum to make sure they were really dehydrated; they didn't care if a woman was around either. Al said, "There's no way that I was going to let those instructors stick that up my butt!" Upon hearing that, I said, "Come here, boy; you are definitely my son." He really hates this story.

It is Al's big day and he told everyone on the ship that he was going to destroy me in tennis. I was invited to tour his ship, the "USS Fletcher" and I met his captain. I was really impressed to be on his ship and I was given a hat with the ship's name on it, which I still treasure.

It was time for the San Diego Open and the boy thought he had the advantage of youth and superior conditioning from the Seal training in his favor. The San Diego Open was over in three days, the least amount of sets that it could happen in. He was devastated, and to add salt to the wound, he had to go back to his ship and tell everyone about his agonizing loss. Al is now the consistent winner in tennis and has acquired many more Opens than me, but never underestimate what a person learns from doing kata.

# The Isshinryuist: A Tale of Endurance

When teaching students about self-defense I tell them you don't have to be the best, but only need to be the best at that moment. A good example of this was when I played tennis in New Hampshire with Al and his friend Ryan, who was a better player than my son. Since there were only three of us playing tennis, two players played against one person, but the "single" player had the double lines to even the odds, otherwise known as "Australian Tennis." I was being badly beaten most of the time because I was playing 8.0 players when both of them were added up. I started to play being the best at that moment and I was up 30-Love. I heard Al tell Ryan, "Don't let him win. I will never live it down." And, yes, I beat them for just one game and this happened just from switching my strategy. This is the way one needs to think when an altercation presents itself. One must be the best at that moment (period).

I played a memorable two and half hour game against a mutual friend of Al and myself. His name was Ken. He was around twenty-four-years of age with little body fat and good muscle tone. He had the build of a professional tennis player. Ken was an A-type personality, which I thought would benefit mankind in some way.

# The Isshinryuist: A Tale of Endurance

I met Ken a few years back in New Hampshire when I went to visit my son there. When I visited Al, I needed to be in A-1 condition just to hang out with him and his friends because there isn't a moment's rest. I also start with a sleep deficit when I get there because of the 12 hours of drive time; on this occasion it was a seventeen-hour drive. We started our day at 6:00 a.m. with some kind of weird workout. We used kettle balls and wiggle gym ropes that were outstretched on the floor, up and down. I didn't work out at 100 percent because after being a cross-trainer most of my life I knew how sore it could make me. Nevertheless, this made no difference because on the ride home from New Hampshire I couldn't turn my neck and I moved like Arnold Schwarzenegger when I turned my shoulders to see the traffic sneak up on me.

Ken did all the exercises at 110 percent and hit the 6:00 A.M. workout four times a week. He looked extremely fit. We played ping-pong and had a fun-filled day and then headed to the bar for cocktails. We closed the bar and Ken and I headed up to his apartment for another brew and some herb; however, we had to ditch my son because he was applying with the FBI or CIA and has never smoked herb. If it were up to me I would make another career choice because of this.

While Ken and I were enjoying ourselves, he told me how big his brother is and the fights that they are always getting into. Suddenly Ken says to me, "I bet you can't choke me out?" My eyes glisten and I'm not sure if he knows that I have studied martial arts for decades, but I am game... He repeats himself and turns around allowing me to put a strangle hold on him. I explain to him that he's too tall and I ask, "If he can bend down a little." When he bends down it makes my heart smile. I have never had anyone give me a golden opportunity to put a choke on him.

I decide on the nut cracker because of the leverage derived from it. He better start taping out immediately because he is going down for the count. This is how it is, no matter who you are. When I apply pressure, he drops his chin and tightens his neck; these are some of the first moves a person makes to defend him or herself. After I feel him do this, I grab his full head of hair and jerk his head back and start to throw him on the floor. Once you work on a person's balance, they forget about everything else, unless they have trained for these moments and are willing to take their fall to stop a successful choke. Ken is not that skilled and I put one hell of a choke on him. He taps out immediately for me to let go.

The next day he comes down to my son's apartment for another day of fun and there are two more mutual friends there, along with my son's girlfriend. Al tells the previous story to his friends, who don't believe him. They ask Ken whether this is true. Ken nods "yes" and they start heckling Ken because I am older and this shouldn't happen to a strong, young man. These friends turn their inquisitiveness to my son and ask him if he can do "that stuff," to which Al nods "yes," which makes me laugh, but I don't say anything.

Sensei Cotton

Sensei Cotton lives in Clarkston, Michigan and I am currently living in Asheville, but I still have business that takes me to Michigan frequently. I train with Sensei Cotton every time I go to Michigan. Sensei showed me a move out of S and T (kata made up by Mr. Johnson). Sensei put the tip of his fingers on my chest very lightly. I somehow thought, "Oh, sensei is being nice to me," but then he exploded burying his knuckles into my chest...the air came out hard. I was done for on this move alone, but sensei had something else planned; the next strike was to both sides of my neck using the thumbs from the Isshinryu fist that are placed on top of the fist. I was amazed that I was still standing and coherent. "Fuck this," I thought. I just wanted go home! It took me a couple of days to figure out where he touched me in the chest and I sure wasn't going to ask him how he did this technique.

Mr. Johnson gave a seminar at Sensei Blate's school, our sister dojo. I was standing next to Sensei Benson who was a good Isshinryu practitioner and worked hard at promoting Isshinryu. He was drafted into the Isshinryu Hall of Fame recently and deserved it for his contribution to the Isshinryu style and his many years of training. Benson was built for fighting. He weighed about one hundred and seventy pounds; he was limber, fast, and hit hard. His kicks were amazing and he was cunning, too. He fought full-contact and I have had my butt kicked by him many times. After fighting Benson I was left lying on the ground in a heap. He would pick me up as though he was giving me a bear hug while he laughed. Most of the time he would knock the wind out of me so hard that I couldn't fake it, that is, fake the fact that I could still breathe. Afterwards, I would have to breathe through my nose for a month because of cracked or broken ribs.

# The Isshinryuist: A Tale of Endurance

Benson used to fight full-contact with a top rated fighter. I was standing next to Benson at an Isshinryu seminar when he first laid his eyes on Mr. Johnson. Mr. Johnson was doing a technique on Sensei Blate. Benson exclaimed, "Where the hell did you find this man?" I used to think sensei Benson was the toughest man alive until I trained with Mr. Johnson and his group.

During the writing of this book, sensei comes to Statesville, North Carolina. He calls me and wants to know if I can train. He prefers for me to meet him in Statesville rather than Asheville, of course, he's sensei. I get excited and tell him that I can be there every night and he stops me by telling me he has too much work to do, but that we can train one night. It is one hundred and eighty miles round trip to Statesville, but it is worth it because Sensei Cotton is a first generation student of Mr. Johnson.

We hug when greeting each other. For the first eighteen years, I didn't even think he liked me. I grab my weapons and we find some shade to start training because it's hot. Sensei can dissect kata and talk about it forever. He can tell you the history of Isshinryu and demonstrate the application (bunkai) and who he has used it on. Sensei's knuckles are like iron. He teaches us that there is pain, but that is the only way a student will understand how the technique works. He is truly an artist. Sensei and I worked out for nearly four hours and then we watched some videos of other Isshinryu karate-ka's afterwards.

# The Isshinryuist: A Tale of Endurance

The best compliment sensei ever gave me was when he asked me to train a black belt who had acquired his Ni Dan (second degree black belt) rank and lived in Tennessee. I never thought he had that much faith in me. One thing Sensei does appreciate is my willingness to train and to be in condition when I arrive. I can empathize with the guy who trains in Tennessee. He is being taught the same stuff that I was taught for nearly thirteen years, which is athleticism.

It's time for me to go back to Michigan to train with sensei. My homage to him is a twelve pack of Sierra Nevada. He likes the IPA and is a microbrewer himself. Currently, he doesn't have a dojo and he usually calls about four or five other Sensei's that he has trained for over twenty five years. We come outside to train if it's nice or in his large living room. The last time I was there he filmed basics for a sensei that noticed him on U tube. As soon as I see the video camera I know that he will want to use me as his uke (they tell us it an honor to be uke), which is another way of saying that you are going get the crap beaten out of you. (I pass this tradition down to the students that I teach as well). He introduces me on the video as a sensei and long-time friend. I am honored. Especially, after all the pain that he has delivered to my body over the decades of working out with him. The reality of it is that he has so much to teach me. The first thing that happens when I see him is a hug and a greeting. After I watch him throw a single punch, I know that I have to work out harder. After all my hard work I still feel that it is in vain and I ask myself: how can this be? What is Sensei doing that I am not catching on to? I train hard and watch videos of: Mr. Johnson and Sensei Rhodes (Mr. Johnson's number one student) and more teachings on tape and videos by Sensei Cotton.

# The Isshinryuist: A Tale of Endurance

The rules for being a good student are to keep your fingers and toenails cut and clean, this must be made a habit. Your gi should be cleaned and pressed. A dojo is a special place and should be treated as such. It is a place where you can leave all baggage behind and concentrate on training. I like the sign Sensei Blate has posted as you enter the door. It states, "Please leave your shoes and ego at the door." Sensei Blate is an excellent sensei and he has a great sense of humor, too. He is a standup character whose benevolence you never want to take lightly.

There are eight kicks taught in Isshinryu basics. I practice one of the kicks from Wansu kata that I teach myself as a basic, but I don't teach this to other students because I don't have the authority to change anything in Isshinryu, nor do I want too. When I hit the dojo floor, I want to be left alone for the most part to train. I hadn't met Mr. Johnson at this point nor had I met anybody that was teaching Isshinryu the way that Shimabuku meant for Isshinryu to be handed down.

Sensei Smith showed up at our dojo. At this point Sensei Cotton had been training under Mr. Johnson for years. In other words, Mr. Johnson's ability flowed through sensei's hands. Under this new lineage I noticed a difference in my Isshinryu within ninety days. I used to spar with Jorge at the hospital and he used to make fun of the way I played tag with him using Sensei Bensons teachings. After training with Sensei Cotton and using Mr. Johnson methods, things changed; when we sparred, there was no more tag. Jorge never sparred with me again. Sensei Smith entered the class thinking that nothing had changed and that he still had top billing, that is, until Sensei Cotton grabbed a hold of him. I haven't seen or heard a person who didn't let out a yelp when Sensei did a hand-seize on the chest after making us let go from a double-lapel-grab.

# The Isshinryuist: A Tale of Endurance

The other noticeable difference in Sensei Smith was that his punches looked weak compared to the days of old. It wasn't that his power had diminished it was that my punches became more powerful while training using Mr. Johnson's method. I never would have believed that sensei would be throwing Sensei Smith around like he did. Sensei doesn't really mean to hurt new students he just doesn't know how hard he hits. A new student doesn't usually make it into the third month no matter how gung-ho they are at the beginning. It's amusing to watch their expression when sensei snaps their elbow the wrong way. Their eyes light up as if they are on fire. After class, they get dressed to go home and we never see them again. We try to convince Sensei Cotton not to put his hands on them for at least six months and let the students become acclimated to the dojo, but he never listens. I guess he wants to see if the student has what it takes to train with him.

The dojo floor is a big room with large mirrors at different ends of the room allowing the student to work in front of them. There is a makawari board (striking post) in the corner. Our best friend is the cement floor, with 12" * 12" tiles over it for padding. There are no mats and we will do anything to get out of a wrist-lock that sensei has applied which includes diving to the cement. I will deal with the pain from the cement later.

After class I was getting dressed in the bathroom with Mr. Snipes. He was complaining that Sensei almost broke his arm; he was really angry and said, "He was going to talk to sensei about lightening up on his technique." I told him, " I don't think he cares whether he hurts us or not.

# The Isshinryuist: A Tale of Endurance

Sensei likes to visit other dojos and was telling me about the time he was getting dressed in the bathroom. A student who was is in there kept saying, "I know you from somewhere," but he couldn't place him until a light bulb went off in his head. He said, "You're the guy that almost broke my fucking arm!" He got dressed hurriedly and headed into the dojo.

Another time, Sensei Cotton was at another dojo exchanging information with a judo practitioner. This man was asking him what you would do if I grabbed you like this. Sensei Cotton said, "Show me." The judo practitioner grabbed a hold of Sensei with a double-lapel-grab and sensei expelled every bit of air out of him after. sensei doesn't need a lot of room to exert power with his technique. I would never want to grab his lapels and leave the soft under-belly unprotected for his pleasure. I look at him as though there is 440 volts flowing through his body and that is something that I don't want to touch.

My body acts like it has a mind of its own when it is cornered by sensei. I tell myself not to yell and don't cower from him. Sometimes, I take aspirin before a workout and have been known to live on aspirin for a week or more while recovering from some of his bunkai demonstrations. This is where he calls you to the front of the class for a public beating in front of all the karate-ka's. You can hear the groans coming from those watching on the sidelines. We all make this "uhh" noise because we are feeling bad for the one who is sacrificing his body for our pleasure. Everyone is mindful that sensei can change the uke's life at the drop of a hat.

# The Isshinryuist: A Tale of Endurance

When we workout it's usually the same protocol. The class meets two nights a week for two hours each night. After the bow-in, we spread out giving room to do punches and kicks. sensei is in marvelous condition and is getting ready to prove it. We start with a few stretches and then he kicks it into high gear. The workout is full of burning muscles, groans and a few students dropping out of line to sit down. When they look as though they are going to faint, Sensei encourages them to sit down. "It is better than hitting your head on the cement floor," he tells us. Many of the new and not so new students take him up on this offer. I have seen sensei retire many karate-ka to chairs, even Sensei Snipes. Sensei Snipes can throw Sensei Cotton around using the hidden secrets of Isshinryu. It's fun to watch him throw sensei around like a rag doll. The only two karate-ka's that sensei has never made sit down during the workouts are Sensei Amstar and myself. Being in shape has always been a top priority for me.

During sensei's workout, aerobics are first and fifty minutes in length. When we stop, my gi is soaked from sweating. The workout starts with jumping jacks, which by itself is already a workout. I try not to breathe through my mouth during jumping jacks. I can see this angers sensei and I know I will pay it for it later. More than likely it will be one of those side line butt-kicking's. This is where he calmly comes over to where I'm working out and just kicks my butt and leaves.

# The Isshinryuist: A Tale of Endurance

After we bow in again, sensei tells us to go to work and we each claim a piece of the floor to do our katas or work with some lower rank student. If we free up sensei's time, he will have more time to work with the upper ranks. When you finish a kata you do another one. You keep busy; sensei doesn't like to see people standing around. If a person isn't working out they will encounter one of his side line butt kicking's; then you will figure out the protocol. You can goof around, but you have to be sly about it. Sensei is always watching the mirrors to see what's happening throughout the dojo. I know the mirrors as well as sensei because of how long I've trained there.

I have been at the front of the line for over a decade. It is the job of a senior Ku (me) to keep the line straight. Everyone in the line is looking at a person's feet to the right to make sure the heels are in line with the senior ku. I am a master at not showing movement while making the line uneven and yelling, "Straighten up the line!" Every time this happens we have to go to the floor and do twenty-five knuckle push-ups. After a few sets of these knuckle pushups the lower ku's are watching my feet because they don't want to do anymore pushups. I do a lot of pushups on my time off because I like having fun with this ritual. Many of the students can't do another pushup and struggle to lift themselves off the floor, but one must try, even if they are unable to do a pushup. They all have a disdain for the muscle burn that I have bestowed upon them. During the workout sensei moves up and down the line standing directly in front of each student punching, kicking and correcting our posture. Sometimes, he stops the class to explain what is happening and how he interprets the move.

Things don't always go right for sensei. There are those unpredictable movements, even for a sensei. When he was working with Mr. VanHeest and showing him some bunkai (Mr. VanHeest is regarded as being clumsy in the dojo and is ranked as second don), he doesn't cooperate and it's not because he doesn't want to; he's just clumsy. Sensei throws him on the floor, but VanHeest hangs on to sensei's gi instead of taking his fall and his elbow smashes Sensei's big toe. Mr. VanHeest weighs a couple of hundred pounds as well. Sensei is jumping around like a chicken with his head cut off. And if there is anything that will send a Frenette into hysterics is another person in pain. This called for a double molar bite on my cheeks to keep from laughing aloud. Even sensei forgot about Mr. VanHeest for a couple of minutes. The color went out of Mr. Vanheest's face and he is extremely pale to begin with. I stand quietly in line and keep the real laughter for later, or it will be me at the end of sensei's knuckles. There is no one to protect you in the dojo. When something funny is happening one has to wait until later to laugh. Sometimes, I laugh for weeks over an episode that happened at the dojo. Mr. VanHeest broke and shattered sensei's big toe, half his foot changes colors. Mr. VanHeest is in trouble and he knows it and so do we. Sensei hobbled for nearly a year and protected his toe throughout the various healing stages.

# The Isshinryuist: A Tale of Endurance

The dojo teaches the student to be aware of his/her surroundings it is part of our training for the world. The main thing to watch for in the dojo is sensei and to see if he is coming in your direction. In my ears, I can still hear his tender words, which sounded like this: "Frenette, I will be dancing down your tonsils!" To which I would reply, "Sensei, I'm not sure what you are so upset about." He would just walk away in disgust. Sensei was teaching Mr. VanHeest the kata Ku San Ku, but VanHeest couldn't grasp it and kept turning the wrong way. Finally, Sensei just started hitting him with his bo in the direction he was supposed to be turning. I lived for these moments; Mr. VanHeest was six feet tall and was always bent at the waist, which made him appear four inches shorter than he really was. I always wanted to tell him to stand straight. When Sensei Snipes was working with VanHeest doing bo/sai kumite, Sensei Snipes hit Mr. VanHeest in the lip with his Sai (mini swords); Mr. VanHeest fell on the floor holding his bleeding lip. Mr. VanHeest wanted to have an ambulance take him to the hospital, but Mr. Snipes told him an ambulance wouldn't be needed since he only needed stitches. Mr. VanHeest wanted to wear his gi to the hospital, but Snipes told him, "You're not wearing your gi to the hospital either." Sensei Snipes drove him to the emergency room for stiches.

The last time I saw Mr. VanHeest he was at the dojo giving away all the things related to Isshinryu. Most of those things went to Sensei. Yes, another karate-ka retires form Isshinryu. Mr. VanHeest even traveled to Okinawa to train with Sensei Tatsusamora. He could have been a good martial artist if he had just spent another decade in training.

# The Isshinryuist: A Tale of Endurance

I was known in the dojo for the nipple shot. We didn't spar under Mr. Johnson's teaching, but we did a lot of one-step kumite. This is when the opponent throws a punch or a kick and you counter. There is no escape from the punch after you or your opponent blocks. Most of them are directed at your chest for practice, using a live target and striking on the right side of the chest to avoid the heart. This is how to fillet a nipple; it is an art that I developed to keep the lower ku's in line. After my block, I would smash the two big knuckles (Urakine) into the nipple with a direct hit and now I have my opponent's attention. I hit the nipple in different directions stretching it outwards. After a few of these strikes, the opponent is trying to grab my hand to stop the impact.

Then there was my buddy Alex, the man with purple glasses, who was a hack; he could never blend with a block and he would just light up the nerves on your forearm causing excruciating pain because of his boniness. This would cause my knuckles to fly into his flesh for revenge. Sensei would beat on him because of this as well. Sensei was showing me how to work a technique correctly. Alex got involved and starts showing sensei how it is done. I start biting my cheek because I know this is going to be good... Sensei tells Alex, "I am the sensei here!" Immediately, Alex retreats to the other side of the dojo moving with small steps, but hurriedly. I keep my composure until sensei leaves.

# The Isshinryuist: A Tale of Endurance

Alex told me a story that took place shortly before he became involved in Isshinryu. He was with two of his buddies and was preparing to fight another guy. They started throwing punches and his adversary nailed him in the nose making both nostrils bleed. His friends convinced him that he got lucky. Again, Alex moved in for the kill when the other guy unloaded on his nose again. He told me it hurt like hell. Once again, his friends tried to convince him that he got lucky and to get back in there. Alex told both of them that he was through. He told them, "If you want some of him, get in there and do it yourself, but I am through." This incident led him to the dojo. Alex was one of those guys who could really take a lot of punishment and few like him will ever enter a dojo.

Sometimes, we met at a bar after working out for beer and conversation. Sensei is a political nut and follows Rush Limbaugh, Fox News and Sarah Palin. He is a true republican. I used to debate different ideas with him, but I would lose later on the dojo floor. He wasn't a very good debater and kept repeating the things he heard from Rush Limbaugh's previous broadcast. Great, more regurgitated information coming at us, I thought. He used the dojo floor to pontificate his views. Usually, it's about gun control and a vehement hate for the Democrat's. I wasn't always this smart about discussing politics with sensei, but after being reduced to a heap on the dojo floor I saw a correlation between the two. He called me a liberal and didn't like the fact that I worked for the Obama Presidential campaign. I don't consider myself a Republican or a Democrat. I just want the best possible person for the position elected. He despised the fact that I could easily take him out of his comfort zone in politics, leaving him sounding like a religious fanatic. When we went to the bar for a birthday celebration, I would talk politics with sensei, but I always kept Alex between us to slow sensei down and allowing him to take the hit. Alex was upset with me because of this antic. He was so used to beating on us and being in a public setting meant nothing to him as far as hitting us.

I was happy that sensei moved away from the face grab. This involves him blocking your punch and a sudden seize to the face. He grabs the flesh of the face in the first bend of his fingers and rolls the rest up into a solid fist. This alone is enough to make the strongest opponent want to get the hell away, but there is more. He attaches his arm to obi (belt) and in one circular movement he has us bent over directly in front of him. We start squealing from the face grab alone. And then the finale: He drops a vicious forearm to the neck, where it attaches the body. It sounds like an orchestra of pain going off in one's head. The eyes twitch back and forth in one's head like crazy. The will to fight leaves you and a retreat is gladly accepted.

Sensei Snipes is tough as nails and it's pretty hard to make him yell, but the face grab and the forearm will do it. Sensei doesn't do a normal forearm strike (and he is being kind to us when he does it). His forearms are enlarged to begin with and when he drops that forearm, he relaxes the hand as though he were trying to touch the far shoulder blade. I have learned most my techniques through pain.

Sensei called me out of line to work some bunkai with him and he wants me to punch him in the head as hard as I can. This is at a later stage of my Isshinryu career, meaning I can punch pretty hard. I throw the punch at his head. He blocks and destroys my arm where my fingers become numb. He yells, "Hit me harder!" I put more on it, but his block destroys my arm, again. This time I can't lift my arm up because it doesn't have any feeling in it. He talks to the class and explains that the harder I punch, the more it hurts me. He instructs me to punch him in the head again. And this time he tells me I'd better hit him hard. Just as I punch, he turns his head to talk to the class. I would have probably knocked him out and shattered his jaw or he may have just laughed. I put a squeeze on my punch, which stops motion and I feel the skin on Sensei's chin against my knuckles. His eyes are wide open and he says, "Thanks, Frenette."

I have lived away from sensei for years at a time, but I keep in touch with him when I am coming to town. He seems happy to see me or hurt me, but I am not sure which one it is. But it's a night filled with learning. On one of the last occasions I saw sensei my son was in Michigan, this is a rare occurrence because we live several states apart. I have asked him many times to accompany me to sensei's, but this time I decided not to call him because of the many unanswered invites; plus, if I showed up with my son, sensei would give me a special beating to impress my boy. I decided to take the Dave approach and thought, "Screw the little bastard," as I heard Dave say so many times. The words resonate good memories of the times we spent together. Soon after, my son calls me and asks if I am going to see Sensei's. I tell him, "Yes." He asks, "Can I go with you?" I say, "Sure." We meet a location close to both of us. Sensei is two hours away because of the traffic and there are plenty of traffic jams in Michigan.

# The Isshinryuist: A Tale of Endurance

Al and I are the first to arrive at Sensei's home. Sensei has watched my son grow-up from the time he was a baby. Al is courteous to sensei because he has been around long enough to know what he can do with his knuckles. Al even uses the Isshinryu fist when confronted, which is rare, because he is fit and muscular. He's smarter than me because he has never let sensei show him anything and has never been hurt by sensei.

Sensei and I hug. It is a special relationship, hard to describe. It is like a father and son relationship. Though he is only a year older, he looks much older...probably from being a direct student of Mr. Johnson and the pain he has withstood from being his student. I never tell anyone my age, in case I get a bonus year.

The regular crew is there and we go through our katas together. Sensei will stop us when he catches an error in our kata. He lets most of the errors go or none of us would make it through the first kata. I have never met anyone who can break down kata like sensei. The only person who could dissect kata better was Mr. Johnson. After katas are over, I know what's next, and I look at my boy and he does, too. It looks as though he is looking around for a comfortable chair because sensei is about to unleash a Pandora's Box on me. It starts out ok until he starts notching up the pain. The punches and kicks are really starting to hurt. We are in his large living room, which is carpeted. There is a huge custom piece of marble in front of the fireplace. You would think that because of the room size most of these techniques would happen over the carpet, but I landed on the marble several times. My judo has taught me how to fall properly. It's a hard surface, but sensei's knuckle's hurt more than the marble. It seems as if he were mad at me as he works his knuckles up and down my ribs, chest, legs and arms.

Now he starts directing his bunkai towards my legs and I know immediately that I won't be able to walk normally for at least three days. If you have never been punched above the knee on the inside of the leg, you are really missing something. After taking four or five punches onto these soft spots, I know when we are through we can have a beer. There is a time frame before the swelling will set in and I definitely don't want to give him the satisfaction of seeing me walk away shuffling inches at a time. We say good-bye and the boy and I jump in the car to go have our last beer together. He mentions that he has gift card for Hooters, so we head over to the restaurant. When we get there, the window of opportunity is over and I can barely walk or move, for that matter. I ask him, "Why didn't you jump in and help me?" He replied, "You seemed to be doing ok because you kept getting up."

I made five wood bo's out of exotic wood; three were made out of Babbinga and two were made out of Yellowhart wood. I gave the Yellowhart bo's to sensei and my friend Terrence. Terrence was so proud to receive his bo that he hung it up in his living room and made some type of plaque describing how he got it and what it meant to him; this really cemented our friendship. The bo's were 1 and 1/8 inches thick, square with large rounded corners and heavy. The best compliment came from Terrence's mother. She told Terrence that it was a work of art. I gave the other bo's to my son and daughter. My daughter, Alysia, uses it while training her dogs. My son used his to climb down mountains and it had giant gouges out of it from the rocks.

# The Isshinryuist: A Tale of Endurance

When I was practicing Isshinryu with sensei in his basement, he did a thrust with his bo to my chest. To relieve the pain, I jumped in the air and for a few moments I was suspended in mid-air stuck against the cinder block wall of his basement with his bo pinning me against the wall. If you're wondering if it hurt, you guessed correctly.

Sensei Cotton's workouts were the same week in and week out. We would do a 45 minute grueling workout, take a break and do kata until one of the sensei's came over to check us out. There was a span of two or three years where Sensei Cotton didn't even work out with us. He was always teaching his future wife, Rita. I always thought that my katas would be better if he had distributed his time evenly around the dojo. Fifteen minutes prior to the end of class we would have to listen to his political agenda or talk about his revered NRA and how we should be able to buy armor piercing bullets because it is our God given right.

While in Michigan I manage to catch Sensei Serf at home. I haven't seen him in years. We talk about Isshinryu and people we knew from the past. Before I know it, we are in his driveway working together and exchanging ideas on kata and tweaking the methods that are to be passed down to others. We are pawns in Isshinryu that have dedicated our lives to training and passing down the art of Isshinryu from Tatsuto Shimabuku. Sensei Serf is an excellent martial artist. I show him my bo and the tonfas that I made. He shows me his weapons and I can see that he likes mine a little better. I have been a carpenter most of my life and I saw a few changes that needed to be added after making a few sets of tonfas. The tonfas that I use will be passed down to my son. I have a big hunk of maple waiting for me to make my final set of tonfas.

# The Isshinryuist: A Tale of Endurance

The method that I use on my weapons to get them silky smooth and where they won't hang up in my hands, is to sand them with 600 grit wet or dry sandpaper for a final sanding and then an application of extra virgin olive oil with a soft clean rag to all the surfaces, especially the ends of my weapons. This will keep moisture from creeping into my treasured weapons. I prefer to train outside, but the weather isn't always cooperative and they need to be refinished because of the rain. This can be done by using the aforementioned practice.

Sensei teaches me about grounding which means weight to the underside. It's during the second-level grounding that he teaches me how to move away from an opponent and leaving the opponent in a position where you can reach him, but he can't reach you. I spent a week trying to figure out this new philosophy using a doorway. I took a mirror to the doorway to work with this principle, but nothing changed. I decide to accept this principle "as is."

When Mr. Johnson explained the second level grounding principle to Sensei Benson he didn't believe it, but soon found out that it was true through Mr. Johnson's punches. When Mr. Johnson demonstrates any type of technique, you don't ask to see it again and any doubts you have are gone. A student of Mr. Johnson asks to see a zero air-punch. Sensei Johnson put his fist against his chest. The student told me that he saw his forearm muscles flex and was thrown back four to five feet and landing on the floor gasping for air. He never ever asked that question again.

# The Isshinryuist: A Tale of Endurance

## Situational Awareness

I enjoyed kumite (sparring) and it has many similarities to tennis. During tennis and kumite the strategies are always being adjusted. At times, these two sports will prompt you to talk to yourself and berate yourself in the process. Tennis is an amazing game. After some matches you end up injured just like you do in kumite (fighting-delete). In tennis and kumite you contend with your opponent's mind as well as his body. In tennis you battle the outside elements, the spin on the ball, your speed, the ground composition and how hard your opponent is hitting the ball. And with both sports you only get one chance. Both sports are a battle of the mind with the body being the major component.

What I liked about kumite is that your opponent in front of you. Isshinryu blocks are made up of many small circle movements which appear to look like one large circular movement. Only a trained student of Isshinryu can pick it out. It took me years of practice to incorporate this into kata and before that it took years for me to understand what sensei was talking about before I could even practice it. Many times I just nodded my head as though I understood what he was trying to convey. An example of leading the mind, when I am next to my opponent I will touch his foot or any other part of his body making him focus on that area and leaving my opponent unable to protect the area where I am about to strike.

I don't play around with Isshinryu because it is meant for self-defense purposes only. Occasionally, I will demonstrate some bunkai to someone who is interested. One of the subjects that sensei frequently talks about is the eight directions. When practicing your martial arts; use the eight directions and notice what happens to your opponent. A little movement goes a long way. If you are using the eight directions correctly, it will nullify the strength of the strongest opponent.

# The Isshinryuist: A Tale of Endurance

There are some important points that I want to bring to your attention: A person with a mean face can't hurt you, it is the technique that hurts. Frequently, you will notice that people get loud and start screaming. Again, this cannot hurt you. It is the technique used, that hurts. When people do this, it is considered saber-rattling and it is done to intimidate you. Another important fact that relates to using small movements, evasions can be less than an inch. If you are making huge movements during the confrontation to evade your opponent, you are taking yourself out of the fight. Now you must concentrate on moving back into the fight. Once you enter the combat zone during a confrontation don't leave the combat zone until it's over, combat zone is four to five inches from your opponent.

There are two parts of your body that don't need any conditioning these are your knees and elbows. Sensei Rhodes talks about the ranking of strikes. He considers the knee to be number one and the elbow number two. In the beginning stages of an altercation say, "Stop it! You're hurting me!" before you strike your opponent. This adds confusion in case it goes to court. After the confrontation, leave the area, especially, if you defeat your opponent.

It's important to stay loose before a confrontation. Before a body is able to move, it must relax. If you are loose, you will have a split-second advantage over your opponent. Another technique I use is the kia (yell). It is designed to short-circuit the brain for a split second and only a trained karate-ka can defend against a kia. Martial arts, is about putting yourself at an advantage and your opponent at a disadvantage. A good example of this can be seen in what I describe as, cement feet. This happens by striking slightly above the hips and setting your opponent's weight on their heels and where they are unable to move. After making cement feet on your opponent you have a half-second to do whatever you need too.

While living in Atlantic City I travel to Michigan to visit sensei. I relish some memorable moments with him. We worked out in his basement with our bo's dissecting our first bo kata; Toke MI No. We begin working on bunkai derived from bo kata. After getting my fingers smacked a few times (it's usually the thumbs that take the brunt of the hits while working weapons, sensei teaches me how to do thrusts against an opponent using the end of the bo. It is really a devastating strike because all your power is focused on a half-inch diameter. If you need to test the power of a bo, take it outside and thrust it against the bark of a tree or against ice.

I showed a friend how powerful the bo is by thrusting it into my galvanized tool-box; it put a hole in it. My friend was impressed and I wish I hadn't done that. One of the things that you need to understand is that your weapons are merely an extension of your hands. To do this, just remove the weapons and practice the weapon's kata with your empty hands. The word karate means "Empty Hands." Again, remember to work your eight angles; your opponent is strong in only two of directions. Always keep your feet shoulder-width apart and keep your feet under your shoulders for balance. You mustn't extend your reach, if you have to reach for your opponent you have no opponent because he can't hurt you and you can't hurt him. You need to learn to close the distance (gap) by using proper stance. Before moving into combat zone keep your opponent at working distance until you are ready to move in for total control.

Mr. Johnson was working with a student at one of his seminars and was showing him how a double-punch works and how to use the bo to strengthen his strike. Mr. Johnson was being kind and trying not to hurt the student. The student tells Mr. Johnson that he's not feeling anything. Mr. Johnson notches up the power. A strike is delivered above the heart and the other to the spleen. Later, the student went to the hospital and spends several days there. Mr. Johnson undoubtedly put some ki into the strike.

If a person is throwing a kick, they can't strengthen their stomach muscles. One of the eight principles that govern Isshinryu is, "Strike when opportunity presents itself." People ask me what you would do in this situation. I reply, "I'm not sure because a strike hasn't been delivered and an opportunity hasn't been presented. An opponent may move an inch and I may have to focus on a different technique because it provides a better opportunity.

# The Isshinryuist: A Tale of Endurance

If you see two people walking towards you in an unknown area, pay very close attention. You should focus on keeping them out of your five-foot circle, which you envision surrounds you. Do this when crossing the street, running, etc. If you keep them out of your five-foot circle, you will never have to go into combat mode.

As I was walking down a large hill in Asheville, I noticed another person going up the hill on the other side of the street. He notices me and crosses the street and changes his direction to mimic my movement. Now he is walking behind me and he probably has a weapon because I am just too big for one individual to want to fight me bare-knuckles. It isn't any different from the animal world.

I want to make sure my assumptions are correct so I cross the street to see what he does. He crosses the street again. I speed up my pace a little to put a few more feet of distance between us and we are nearing the darkest area of the street at the bottom of the hill, a spot where things may happen... At this point, I run up the hill as fast as possible. Hill running is one of my strengths and will allow me to be out of harm's way. I never look back until I get to the top of the hill, and when I do, he's gone. In certain situations, I will go to the car and untuck my shirt as though I put a gun in my pants. When I see two people split up while I am walking towards them, I know that this is probably not a good scenario. I handle this situation by bending over and pretending to grab a rock (man's oldest weapon). I position my hand where the rock is hidden in the palm of my hand because most of the time, I can't find a rock that quickly. The person in question will cross back over to the other side of the street thinking that I have an advantage.

# The Isshinryuist: A Tale of Endurance

While working in the slums of Highland Park and ripping the boards off of an old, abandoned building that was previously owned by a former auto executive, a lady yells out from across the street, "They cut a dog's head off and stuck it on a stick and out the window of that house last week." These weren't reassuring words when I'm about to enter the house with a flashlight, paper and pencil in hand. When dealing with drug addicts, I know that most of them will not have weapons or guns because they sell everything of value to buy drugs. If a fight ensues, it will be a hand-to-hand combat or with simple weapons (whatever is lying around on the ground).

While I was in a four-story building that has no electricity and very little light because it is boarded up, the first thing I do is grab a stick in case there is a dog. More than likely I will have to make several trips back here spending hours each time inside the house before completing my construction write-up. I always yell first to give whatever is in the building a chance to clear out or hide, always hoping for the first scenario. Hearing is your most important asset. The basement is the most concerning and that is why I save it for last. I do not want to be trapped down there while someone ponders my demise.

My fighting stance starts in a neutral position with my feet poised at shoulder width apart and under my shoulders. This stance does not concern an opponent because they do not know what a person can do from this position. I didn't discover this fact on my own; I learned it from watching Mr. Johnson do bunkai on his uke and going over his positions in my mind. For years I wonder, "Why does he stand this way? And then one day I had an epiphany. I'm amazed that I can attack, evade and hit all eight angles nullifying my opponent's strength. Stance (always) gives me an advantage over my opponent.

# The Isshinryuist: A Tale of Endurance

I started working out in an Isshinryu dojo near Peoria, IL. It was run by Sensei Runyon who invited me to train with him, but he had left on a trip when I arrived at his dojo. It is located in a bar where the patrons are one floor above us and can watch us train behind a bluish tempered glass. I forgot they were there, once I started working out. There is a fourth-don leading the class. He picks out bunkai from kata and then tries the moves on the students, everyone struggles with the moves. After I introduce myself, I find a vacant spot on the gym floor. Nothing takes the place of training. If you attain the rank of Shodan (black belt), your journey is just beginning. If you plan to excel at martial arts, you need to keep yourself motivated in order to train. One of the ways I accomplish this is by reading the biographies of famous people and fighters. You will find one common connection with most famous people, whether it's a fighter, a president, a general or an explorer; they have the heart of a lion and never give up. This doesn't mean you won't have failures. Failures are inevitable and set backs are to encourage you to do better.

When I go to seminars and train with other martial artists, I don't try to remember the entire seminar, but instead I take home a few good points and incorporate them into my martial arts. The same with reading, I gather a few good points from every book striving for continuous improvement (kaizan). The quote that has influenced me the most in my martial arts journey comes from the book "Raging Bull" by Jake LaMotte. He wondered how people can go through life without a passion. He says, "I have a dream and only one dream and that is to be the middle weight champion of the world." Everything Jake did is aimed at making his dream a reality.

I have two children. The one thing that have I passed down to them is to have a passion. My daughter is a professional dog trainer, breeder and owns three German Shepherds. She studies Schutzund, a way of teaching dogs to attack using German commands. She loves animals so much that she will wear anyone out talking about this subject.

My son's passion is fitness, tennis and the great outdoors and he is every bit as passionate about these as I am about my martial arts. When he was in high school he wanted to become a Navy Seal. He started swimming as soon as the ice started breaking up. He was accepted into the Seals and made it to "hell week," but had to quit as many other applicants do. His reason was shin splints. His failure fueled his future dedication towards a different passion. I was overjoyed that he didn't make it as a Navy Seal. I didn't raise him to become cannon-bait. His job in life is to take care of me in old age and I hope he agrees.

# The Isshinryuist: A Tale of Endurance

## Sensei Blate

I liked working out with Sensei Blate, who is currently president of the Okinawan Karate Association and a great storyteller. While in his class, he talks about the time he was doing a Tamashiwari (Breaking) demonstration for kids at an elementary school. He uses his two big knuckles (Urekin) for many of his breaks. His encore consists of breaking eight inches of concrete slabs with his open hand with no spacers using a soft technique. Afterwards, he notices all the kids are laughing and snickering at him while his hand is hurting; this is when he realizes the kids are smarter than him and gives up this practice.

On TV I see martial artists break huge blocks of ice and wonder why they do it and how. I would rather hit my opponent a few more times than do this. I punched a locker in front of three or four people (while working at the hospital) and broke my middle knuckle. In an instant, my knuckle swelled as large as Sensei Benson's golf ball sized knuckles. My co-workers look at my hand, but I pretend that it doesn't hurt. After this incident, I was unable to reach inside my front pocket for six months. Later I look at the locker and see two small dings in it thanks to my knuckles. I open the locker and the label reads "Explosion-proof." "Damn, "I sure can do some dumb stuff." When entering the dojo sensei sees my hand and reprimands me for hitting a hard object. He says, "Do you want to have crab hands when you get older?" Later he teaches me the proper use of a working Makawari board (punching post).

# The Isshinryuist: A Tale of Endurance

Sensei Blate creates laughter while leading calisthenics, but his demeanor could change in a second and make us fear for our life. One time I smoked weed on my way to class. Sensei Blate asks, "I smell smoke. Is that you Frenette?" "It's not me, sensei," I reply. Later that night, when we spar with Sensei Blate, he put a beating on a student that he believes is the weed smoker. This student's lips and nose were bleeding. He tells him to, "Get something to clean up that blood." I imagine this student is becoming a better fighter because of me, but I never see him again. The truth is that I didn't want to lie about the weed, but I did so to save my hide.

Sensei Blate was a vice president at a mid-size underground utility company. He held a high-level meeting and his boss embarrassed him during the meeting. Afterwards, he went into to the president's office and told him that if ever did that to him again, "I will beat you to near death and then resuscitate you and do it (beat you) again." His courage to speak his mind cost him his job. After this incident he does not mope around, but moves forward. I study management and believe that most of the world's woes are because of bad managers holding the exclusive right to ruin someone's day just because they can.

# The Isshinryuist: A Tale of Endurance

As I was leaving the dojo and grateful for not being hurt by Sensei Blate, I was bowing when Sensei Blate wanted to show me something. He had me grab his wrist and demonstrated a release. I saw his obi (belt) move and I heard a pop come from my wrist setting off a loud yell. Afterwards, I thanked him and completed my bow. When I jumped in the tuck I examined my wrist and I was concerned whether it was broken and if I needed to go to the Emergency Room. I drove away using one hand. When I arrived at one way street in Pontiac, I went the wrong way because I was thinking about my wrist. Immediately, the sirens went off and I was pulled over. I didn't want a ticket and told the officer that I just left Blate's Karate School and told him about my wrist. I was hoping to avoid a ticket. He knew Sensei Blate and sympathized with me and let me go.

How the nipple shot was born... Sensei Blate has extremely fast hands. I have only met three people that have hands faster than most and Mr. Johnson was one of them. Sensei Blate was asked to drive other peoples' car for races because of his hand speed. Sensei Blate was in front of me and said, "Frenette, I am going to punch real slow and I want you to block it. He punched and I barely moved before his big knuckles smashed my nipple with me thinking "fuck that hurt." The nipple is screaming!!! This time he tells me, "am going to punch you again and I want you to block it." My nipple is telling me, you better protect me. He throws a punch, I barely moved my arm again, but this time, he the same nipple twice. That nipple swelled, leaving with the "Nipple Shot!" This is my punch for future use against other students while doing one step-kumite.

### Sensei Rhodes

I was talking to Sensei Snipes about the upcoming seminar that Sensei Rhodes was putting on, who is Mr. Johnson's number one student. After Mr. Johnson's death he took over his dojo, and is traveling around the US and Canada and sharing his knowledge through seminars. They are conducted in other sensei's dojos. The home dojo sponsoring Sensei Rhodes would use Friday night for weapons training and it was only open to them. Saturday, is open to everyone and all types of styles, ranks or age within reason. The people attending these seminars were usually high ranking dons from many different styles that brought a few of their students too.

On this day Sensei Snipes was telling me about the time he was uke (partner) for Sensei Rhodes. He described how Sensei Rhodes hit his jaw with his open palm and then flipped the same hand over creating a quick back fist to cheekbone. He said, "It hurt!" I arrive at Sensei Rhode's seminar. When we bowed in, there were probably thirty students attending. Sensei Rhodes demonstrates Wansu kata and then pulls pieces out of the kata to demonstrate how to apply these moves into (bunkai) application. We take turns being his partner for demonstrative purposes.

# The Isshinryuist: A Tale of Endurance

When we break for lunch, I see an opportunity to talk to Sensei Rhodes while nobody is around. We start discussing Isshinryu and in the next second he is jacking my jawbone with the palm of his hand and then a back fist to my cheekbone with his conditioned knuckles, I feel my cheek begin to swell. Sensei Snipes was right, it did hurt. I tell him that it's a nice technique. He tells me a story where he is at his dojo and a sensei wants to bring his MMA fighters to spar with him, he agrees to work out with them. Next week, three no-neck opponents show up to spar. Sensei Rhodes explains to them how he practices. He asks one of them to throw a punch and punishes him to the oak floor. He practices on another MMA fighter allowing him to throw a punch-kick combination, duplicating the same results. They tell him they don't fight like that and he tells them to do what your used too. Sensei Rhodes takes another one out. They leave and never show up at his dojo again. I am not sure why, but he seemed to take to me and told me more stories…

Sensei Rhodes told me about an episode with Mr. Johnson and as they were getting dressed, Mr. Johnson told him to seize one his love handles and squeeze, he is squeezing with all his might. Mr. Johnson says is that all you have and he squeezed even harder. Mr. Johnson grabs him by his chest and puts a squeeze on Sensei Rhodes that makes him let go. When he gets home, his wife was in bed and she notices from a dim light that he is really hurt as he is undressing. She blurts out, "Oh my God, what has that man done to you, now." Sensei Rhodes was telling me that after Mr. Johnson died it took three years before some of his body parts were beginning to heal.

# The Isshinryuist: A Tale of Endurance

Mr. Johnson sponsored an annual week-long seminar at his dojo every August. I have never been there and I made it a point to visit his dojo. Sensei Rhodes has kept the tradition alive. The doors are left open all week for you to come in and train and this is the main event. People fly in from all over the world to come to this seminar. I am living in San Antonio Texas which means it expensive with airfare, lodging, meals, car rental and the price of admission.

I have been told how hot it gets at the seminar and nobody is going to see me sit in a chair because it's too hot or because of lack of conditioning. I even hit the weights and I despise lifting weights. After two weeks of counting; one, two, three, I injure my back and give up the weights, its three weeks before the seminar and hopefully, I will have time heal. I am training in a racquetball court and the air conditioning isn't working either. Believe me it's hot, this is Texas. I train here four days a week and I am glad the air isn't working. This will ensure that I have stamina to accept the heat in Iowa with little or no problem. My student trains with and me and never complains about the heat, plus, he works in the sun all day, too.

When I arrive at the dojo no one is there. I take a walk to loosen up and to receive some cool air on my skin. When I arrive back at the dojo Sensei Rhodes is there and we hug. I have known him for years. The next thing I do is walk around taking everything in and taking photos of everything for my future dojo. He has pictures of Mr. Johnson and Shimabuku. I have been in martials arts for nearly forty years and I never seen a better martial artist than Mr. Johnson. But the one thing that could piss him off was to call him master. The reason being is that Isshinryu can never be mastered.

# The Isshinryuist: A Tale of Endurance

I help Sensei Rhodes set up for the seminar. I see a lot old acquaintances and meet new ones too. Anybody that looks at my belt can tell that I have been training a long-time. I am Sempi to most people, which means, "He who came first." Many of the students have never met Mr. Johnson, since, he died twelve years ago and they love the first hand stories that I have of him.

Sensei Rhodes bows us in. We are split up into two groups. I join the side with Sensei Rhodes while Sensei Cotton teaches the other group empty hands and history. I want to stay as close as possible to Sensei Rhodes. Sensei Torey is teaching Sensei Rhodes weapons (Kuboda) and is leading our group. After lunch we start bunkai. Sensei Rhodes is brutalizing us and giving bruises for free. I am working with Sensei Torrey and he tells Sensei Rhodes that he is having trouble making the bunkai work on me. Sensei Rhodes takes me center stage to demonstrate. I have eaten aspirins twice today already. He has me punch and hits my forehead with his forearm from no more than two inches away and an instant fucking headache occurs and I want to go home. This is no fun at all. Then he does it again. The next strike was to my rib, but I was still upstairs, concerned with the headache. Afterwards, we bowed out and I wanted to be as far away from him as possible. This is why he is Mr. Johnson's number one student.

# The Isshinryuist: A Tale of Endurance

Sensei Rhodes was studying Kung Fu when he had met Mr. Johnson. It was at a martial arts exhibition where different styles were doing demonstrations and trying to sell gi's and accessories. But the main reason for being there was to recruit new students. Sensei Rhodes was there with his table doing the same. He knew of Mr. Johnson, but had never worked with him or seen him workout. In comes Mr. Johnson wearing his gi and pushing a wheel barrow filled with bricks, wood and cement for a breaking demonstration. Sensei Rhodes noticed Mr. Johnson kept looking at his watch. Later, he comes over to the Kung Fu table and asks, "If his partner didn't show up could he help him out. Sensei Rhodes says, "Sure Mr. Johnson anything you need, be glad to help." It started out with them holding stuff while Mr. Johnson broke objects with his knuckles.

When his uke didn't arrive, he asked Sensei Rhodes to be his uke. Sensei Rhodes remembered facing Mr. Johnson when he saw Mr. Johnson's eyes show some white and after that he woke up on his back. He got up and Mr. Johnson proceeded to use him as a mop. When he left the stage the uke who supposed to be there was clapping. He was telling Sensei Rhodes that he had never seen anybody get there ass kicked like that. After that Sensei Rhodes started training with Mr. Johnson.

Saint Croix Housing

The Virgin Islands was approximately twelve hundred miles south of Miami. I walk onto the public housing community that I am hired to manage and I'm disheartened to see a community that looks like a war zone. I walk the entire site and around every building. There is litter everywhere: paper, bottles, discarded old bikes lying behind apartment units and red grocery carts lying sideways on rooftops. The grass hasn't been mowed in weeks. I was hired to manage two communities. JFK has two-hundred family units and Ruby is a Senior Citizens Community with thirty-five units that doesn't have much happening, except for neighbors squabbling and water pipes breaking every now and then. JFK covers nearly three city blocks and includes a ball field, a basketball court and a community room. There are no less than forty cars parked on the grass and roads encircle the buildings making it look like a Go-Kart track from the residents driving on it. There are groups of muscular teenagers and gang-bangers hanging out everywhere. It is extremely hot. I have visited places known for hot weather, such as Florida, California and Nevada, but this heat feels different, it's an oppressive heat. As I enter the community, I see a worker driving a golf cart and getting out too pick up trash. I ask him how many units there are in this community, but he won't answer. He turns out to be Jonas, a man nearing seventy-two who is an excellent carpenter and is one of my best workers.

# The Isshinryuist: A Tale of Endurance

As I walk around greeting the residents, they appear dumbfounded to see a "white person" walking around the community. The word is out that I am the new manager. In a few moments I am surrounded by people asking questions trying to figure out if I am going to be a difficult manager. The next few weeks are different. I take a lot of FU's from the residents, but I never let anyone get away with it without a verbal confrontation. And you haven't been chewed out until you have pissed off a black lady. I have been known to take a woman or two, to lows that they didn't even know they could go too from my personal life alone.

I'm starting work in a few days and I need to find a place to shower or swim before work, because I don't have a place to stay. Luckily, I have an adapter that plugs into my car lighter making it possible to iron my clothes on the hood of my car. I can hear the Crucian's (natives to St. Croix) say as they watch me, "What is that foolish, white boy up to?" I am spending four hundred on a rental car a week until mine arrives. It will cost another thousand for a place to live. I am happy that I'm able to adhere to this routine for a month until my car arrives. Earlier on, my wife said, "I will put your title in a safe place." It is nowhere to be found… She really loves me and cut my phone off in Puerto Rico because it may cost her some money. At least I got my last call out to General Motors securing the title before she did that. And a phone would have been nice because I didn't have a clue about anything on St. Croix. Every word I mutter is a question. And it starts with do you know where…

# The Isshinryuist: A Tale of Endurance

I lived on the east side of the Island, where the winds drive the heat and the sands from Africa making this side of the island a desert. The other side of the island is a tropical rain forest. It seems strange to have such variations in climate in less than a thirty mile radius. The plant life here includes cacti, agave and aloe vera. Iguana lizards and mongooses can be seen everywhere. Mosquitoes control the island and some are so small they go through screens. The island is approximately nine miles in width and thirty miles in length. It takes nearly three hours to travel from one end to the other. The longest area stretches from East to West. There are torrential rainfalls in St. Croix. The roads are worse than the ones I remember driving while being in Mexico, though the speed limits are low. It is common to see goat herds and chickens crossing the road while driving and an occasional horse. I never realized chickens were smart until I lived here. They run from cars...

There are many hair-pin curves that caused my belongings to go airborne in the process. I feel like a race-car driver. While living in North Carolina I thought mountain driving was tough, but it's worse here. This reminds me of the way people would drive in Africa (no stop lights) and we drive on the left in St. Croix. I am always stopping to let a car in or out. One of the nice things about living on St. Croix is that there aren't any snakes, thanks to the mongooses. They were first introduced on the island to combat the rats that eat the sugarcane. It wasn't a well-thought-out plan because the rats are nocturnal while the mongooses are diurnal. The mongoose looks like a miniature dinosaur with a mouth that can open up so wide and looks as if its jaw will unhinge.

# The Isshinryuist: A Tale of Endurance

After being educated by Ms. Strawberry the Human Resource Manager and signing all the new-hire documents, I am sent to my community, Here I meet my crew, except for my maintenance foreman (Somali) who is on vacation, which means I have to do my job and his job as well. I also meet Ms. Gumbo and Tonita, my office staff. Tonita is a petite, well-mannered and friendly. Ms. Gumbo is nice and helpful at first, but later she shows her true colors. She hates Somali and tells me his faults. Every time she opens her mouth it's to say something derogatory about him. Somali doesn't care for Ms. Gumbo either, though he doesn't harbor the intense hatred that Ms. Gumbo does. When I am out in the community, I ask the Crucian's, "Have you seen Somali, he is a handsome dark-skinned man that looks like he needs a meal." This always makes them laugh.

I take a moment to examine the facts. Somali works every moment of the day while Ms. Gumbo is on the Shopping Network and Facebook a large part of the day. The community dislikes Ms. Gumbo and they refer to her as, "That big, fat, fucking, black bitch." Her opinion of everyone living in the community is that they all have game (scams). Her customer service skills are non-existent.

I nick-name Ms. Gumbo "The owl" because her neck turns in such a way that one would think she has 140 neck-bones just like an owl. Her flexible neck allows her to see everything that goes on in the office. When she sees something wrong, she calls or emails Mr. Swanson (my boss).

Mr. Swanson invites me, along with Ms. Strawberry and Petunia (Mr. Swanson's secretary) to the central office to visit a few sites. The ladies are seated in the front of the SUV while Mr. Swanson and I are seated in the back. Because I am a new employee, I am ready to ask him questions about the agency and about him. However, when I ask a question, he doesn't respond. He seems more interested in tapping his leg with his fingers to the tune of a song he has stuck in his head.

After driving by a couple of housing sites, they order lunch to-go. I don't get anything to eat because I don't eat red meat. When we are ready to leave, we can't find Mr. Swanson. He is visiting a street vendor on the corner. When he gets in the SUV, he directs his attention to the ladies in the front seat and asks, "Do you know what she's selling?" "No," they respond. Mr. Swanson says, "She is selling Hoochie-Powder. Do you know what that is?" Again, the ladies' response is, "No." Mr. Swanson can barely contain himself and excitedly blurts out, "It helps tighten your vagina." The situation doesn't improve when he proceeds to tell Ms. Strawberry, "I bet you need two packages." He is rolling back and forth in his seat laughing uncontrollably. This is unprofessional conduct at its best. The women aren't laughing, but somehow manage to crack a forced smile. I just want to get out of the SUV because I don't want to be involved. Considering that Ms. Strawberry is our Human Resources Director, one would think that Mr. Swanson would be reprimanded or fired for his inappropriate comments, but she does absolutely nothing, but smile.

Every day is filled with resident's complaining even if I had heard the same complaint the day before. When I put myself in their shoes, their grievances are legitimate. None of the units have air conditioning or hot water. Most of the screens have holes in them and there are no screen doors that would allow them to open the exterior door to get some relief from the heat. The exterior doors are left wide open allowing mice and rats to enter the units causing more problems. The simple solution is to provide security screening that doesn't tear easily and lasts many years.

While walking through JFK, it reminds me of a bombed-out area in the Middle-East. The tenants throw their trash and food scraps off the back porch, which attracts rats and flocks of chicken. When addressing this problem, the tenant on the top would point to the person on the bottom and the tenant on the bottom would blame the tenant on the top. I give up! It's a hopeless situation.

A common scenario at Housing Authority is as follows: A single mother that is on a housing waiting list will come into the office to sign a lease for an apartment; most of the time she is employed. Within thirty days she will lose that job and come to the office to ask for a hardship adjustment, though in reality she will become a credit renter. This apartment can be viewed as finding a gold mine: If she doesn't have a car, someone that can provide one, will live with her. If she needs cash, someone will move in to fulfill that need. It's a vicious cycle. The mother now receives a check to live there, allowing her to party all day, sleep in, except to put her kids on the bus. She now has more spendable income than if she was working. There is an easy solution to this problem; have a lawyer give her an eviction notice addressing the people that aren't on the lease. The attorney now knows every detail of the case, and after a few evictions the young ladies won't be so willing to let someone move into their apartment. Usually, the people that cause the majority of the problems in the housing authority are the ones that are staying there illegally.

Ms. Gumbo holds her first resident meeting. It turns out to be the most chaotic meeting I have ever witnessed, with everyone talking amongst themselves and no one listening. A fight even breaks out. The following meeting, I take charge and ask, "How is everyone doing on this fine, hot day in paradise? I tell them, "This meeting will be a little different, if anyone is here to pick up a utility check, please come and get it and you are excused from the meeting." Everyone behaves and the meeting is short and productive. I had lots of arguments with the residents, but afterwards, we are friends because they know that I am there to help them. Many of them approach me later to apologize.

The HUD inspection is getting closer and Mr. Swanson calls asking for a tour of the property. He requests a golf cart be made available for his use. We haven't had a maintenance person around here in weeks. What does he think is going to be different since his last visit? I see a gentleman driving a small, white van. He comes through the community selling bread, cheese and fruit pasties. I purchase two agave pasties and ask him to put the pasties in separate white bags. This gentleman is always pleasant and saves me the trouble of going out to grab a five-minute lunch somewhere. Now I'm off to find a golf cart. We have two golf carts for the community because it is so large, but I always walk. Completing work orders for the residents is my main objective. It's amazing how a golf cart can hide when you need one. I am late because I can't find one and Swanson didn't give me much notice either. I am hustling to meet him, not because I am worried about him, but because he's a screamer, like a drill sergeant in a boot camp and I have to listen to it.

I can tell he's irate, but that's to be expected. He is standing there waiting for my arrival. To add some fun to the golf-cart tour, I am going to drop this golf cart off a curb to make his teeth slam. For as long as I have lived I awarded Mr. Swanson the distinction of being the biggest jackass I have ever met. As I pull up next to him I say, "Hi, Mr. Swanson, I bought you a pasty." He is stunned at my generosity. He climbs in the golf cart. It's hard for me to pretend that I like someone when I don't. He talks incessantly, sometimes, I feel like asking him, "Don't you take time to breathe?" He is waving at people and smiling at the ladies. In reality, he's about as popular as "Chicken Pox". The residents know that since he arrived, he hasn't done a thing for this community. I wave at the ladies and they respond with smiles and greetings. They sneer at Mr. Swanson. During this visit, he gives out so many orders it would take twenty maintenance workers to complete the work. This fool thinks he's General Patton, but instead of driving around in a jeep, he's riding in a golf cart. He has the audacity to ask me to give all the keys to an on-call person that I have never met. When I refuse, he threatens me with a write-up and time off without pay. My response: If that is what you need to do, fine. I am responsible for everything that happens within these 235 units and it isn't going to happen on my watch.

With my position, it seems that I would drive around in a decent company vehicle. The first vehicle keeps overheating and stranding me in remote places. I had to ride in a tow truck twice. The next vehicle is even worse. It's a small, blue Chevrolet pick-up with lots of power and four bald tires. The air conditioning doesn't work and the only window that rolls down is the passenger window. The seat is destroyed and the metal showing can cut you. I always wondered what a steering wheel looks like without the plastic covering, but not anymore. I cleaned out the first vehicle until it shined, but I am not about to clean out this death trap, except for washing the windows. This little, blue pick-up has no rear-view mirror or one the door on the driver's side. Most of the personnel refuse to drive it. It stalls every time it comes to a stop. During a rainstorm I find out that the wiper on the driver's side spins continuously which makes me pull off the road until it stops raining.

Mr. Swanson is in the states and Ms. Gumbo keeps him informed through phone and emails him regularly. This means he calls me and I get yelled at military-style. I didn't volunteer for the military when I was nineteen and I am not signing up for it now.

# The Isshinryuist: A Tale of Endurance

The holidays on St. Croix are equivalent to a mini Mardi Gras. The Crucian's put large speakers on the back of a pickup (Tram) and the entire neighborhood surrounds the truck. The resident's follow the truck smoking Gongi and drinking rum, while someone MC's from the back of the truck with a microphone. Its 9 a.m. on Saturday when the tram shows up in front of the dojo where I am training. Through its loudspeakers, I hear, "Larry the manager, Larry the manager. Come on out." I know they won't leave unless I do. Dressed in my Gi, I step outside. The men shake my hand; the women hug me and the kids run around while they yell my name out. It's really quite touching.

I train in the community room after work and on the weekends. The residents enjoy this because it gives them more time to get their mail and to make a report, if there is something wrong in their unit. I never worry about my car being damaged or anyone accosting me as I walk around the community at night. They like seeing me around the community. Many times I have to cut our conversations short, which upsets them; they don't realize that, by that time of night, it has been a long day. I talk to them as they smoke their Gongi (weed) and drink beer. I never smoke or drink beer with them. I encounter various groups while walking around to ensure the community is secure. During these walks we talk about politics and many different issues. But it wasn't always like this. I had to earn their respect and walking around at night does just that. At first they give me dirty looks and would throw something on the ground and say, "Pick up my trash white boy." It's easy to be mean when you don't know someone's name.  After I learn their names and earn their trust, things change.

Occasionally, I would slip the kids a twenty. They like it and it makes me feel good. I go to the swing set and give the kids an "underdog." This is where I push the swing a few times and tell them to hang on. Then I run underneath the swing and yell, "Underdog." The line keeps getting longer until I finally have to set a cutoff point. The kids know I train every evening in the community center so they show up at the door, four persons deep. I never let them in the community center, but I let them watch. I open the door and lock the iron-gate. I'm not sure how it all started, but I'd walk over to the gate and there were four kids on the other side of it. I'm holding my bo. I ask them, "Have you ever seen this before?" They answer, "No." I take the Bo and swing it over the top of their heads as hard as I can. They looked like a deer-caught-in-the-headlights. Fear overtakes them as my bo makes a thunderous sound on the horizontal bar and stopping just a few inches above their heads. After their fear subsides, they start to laugh. The first time I swung the bo at that bar I impressed myself because I didn't know I could hit so hard. The kids enjoy this stunt so much that they bring their unsuspecting friends over so I can scare them as well.

I have a student who shows up for lessons. His name is Lanki and he's done some boxing in the past. He seems pretty fit and strong from being a weight-lifter. I start by teaching him how to hold his fist and how to walk and to punch correctly. I demonstrate push-ups on the marble floor of the community room. I explain that I only want to see two marks on his big knuckles (Urakine) when he gets up after doing push-ups. The results from Lanki's efforts result in zero push-ups, but they produce lots of grimacing. Lanki confides to me that the word in the community is that, "Larry ain't scared of nothing." In the beginning I usually took my first "Fuck You" at 7:20 a.m. He shows up for three or four lessons and then decides he doesn't care for the pain associated with learning Isshinryu.

# The Isshinryuist: A Tale of Endurance

Before I started working at the community, gun play was prevalent here. The first time guns were used was when gang members were committing robberies using a machine gun. They became bold enough to commit these crimes during the day. At least eight police in SUVs arrive at the scene. These SUVs were the largest that I have ever seen. The police were carrying machine guns and wore bullet proof vests. They spread out and were swaying their guns back and forth as though in a war zone. One cop stood on the roof of his vehicle and was pointing his gun at the tenant's windows. (The tenant buildings are three-stories-high with most buildings having twelve units.) I usually go and talk to the police and ask them why are you parked on my grass, but this wasn't the time. After handcuffing a couple of perpetrators, the police vanish along with the suspects. The residents are enraged. Most Crucian's aren't fond of the police, who have a questionable reputation after years of corruption on the island.

The party starts a five o'clock on Friday. The music starts blasting and I mean blasting and out come's the beer, the rum and the Gongi. The Rasta's are natives to the island and some work with me. Smoking weed is part of their religion, so I don't interfere. It's no different than what is done in the white community, except that it isn't done so openly.

While I was working there someone got shot and was taken to the hospital. The next shooting is a major one and it unfolds before my very own eyes and from less than two hundred feet away. The shooting happened while I was fixing exterior lights. I heard gunfire and headed towards the office to investigate.  I see a man come running out of a unit from where I am standing. I watch as he empties a gun that he had hidden in a magazine. The gun could pass for a 45. He was wearing a green t-shirt that was pulled over his head exposing only the golden triangle (the weak part of the skull) to allow vision but to avoid detection.  He is preoccupied with the other shooter, who hasn't fired back yet, my first instinct is to run up from behind and tackle him. The two things that stop me from acting on this, is that I am wearing steel-toed boots, which will reduce my speed and it is uphill and bullets started flying from the person who was being shot to begin with. The first shooter ran away fast. I enter the office and Tonita and Ms. Gumbo are gone. I go to the maintenance shop and send everyone else home as well. I go back to changing some lights and train in the community center, afterwards. The next day, I speak with the families of both shooters to inform them that the shooters are not allowed back in the community. After our war-of-words one family moves out while the other family does likewise after receiving an eviction letter. I inform everyone that gun play will never be tolerated and that they will not be allowed to live here.  The message sinks in and gun shots are never heard again in our community.

# The Isshinryuist: A Tale of Endurance

After the last shooting, the grandmothers of the shooters begin to quarrel amongst themselves. Keep in mind that these women have to see each other every day and both shooters come from side-by side units. One lady tells me that the other resident confronted her in downtown Christiansted and was shouting out profanities at her. I ask, "You mean the way you cuss me out for asking you to move your car off the grass?" She replies, "Yeah, just like that". After one of them received a black eye there hasn't been a problem between them.

I greet many Crucian's from their balconies and wave to them as I venture off to the Central Office. There are people that wave at me while standing in front of the grocery store inviting me to come over, but this time I wave back and keep going. I run into more tenants. One lady is cute; I recognize her as the woman who made advances at me earlier saying, "I wore this outfit just for you." I just brush them off because I follow a code of ethics: If you don't want your family, friends or relatives to see it in the newspaper, then don't do it. Another lady named Dolores, who is eighty-years-old grabs, my hands while talking to me. On one occasion, she grabs my butt and says, "I want to see that white ass." I laugh and move on.

Mr. Swanson comes over to visit a unit and things aren't going well. He has everyone working on other sites, leaving no one available to work on this unit. When we arrive at the unit, my maintenance man is there. Mr. Swanson starts to scream at me as if I were a little kid. "Is this how you manage, Frenette?" "Yes it is," I answer. He screams out, "This unit will be finished before I come back in the morning, no excuses, and I don't' care how you do it. I am thinking about kicking Humpty-Dumpty's behind and throwing him off the third floor balcony. But, then I remember what sensei said to me, "If you can beat him in your mind, there is no need to fight."

The next day Mr. Swanson comes back and talks to my maintenance man, Jeremy, who tells him that all we were able to do is put glue down. Then he calls me to ask me about the unit. I explain that "I do not have any additional information, other than what Jeremy gave you." Mr. Swanson says, "But I am asking you and I don't need an attitude." My response is, "Neither do I." The next time, I see Mr. Swanson and Ms. Strawberry they inform me that I didn't make my six months' probation. The residents were shocked and can't believe that they are letting me go because of my work ethic. I hear the tenants yell my name out as I drive through town as if I were a celebrity. After I was let go, I met up with one of the residents. She tells me that that there is graffiti written on the sidewalk and walls of the office at JFK, right in front of the spot where Ms. Gumbo parks her car. It reads: "Big, Fucking, Fat, Black Bitch: we are going to kill you, burn your car, burn the office and we know where you live." Another piece of graffiti reads: "We want Larry back." Though amusing, I don't condone this type of behavior. The residents praise all the accomplishments that took place while I was there. They also mentioned that, "There used to be a lot of turf wars between the gangs, where others couldn't go, but since I came, all that ended." It made me feel good that residents felt this way about me. Another resident says, "I have been without lights in my archway (entrance to her home) for years, that is, until Larry arrived, and he repaired them on the weekend." She also mentions that, "The whole community hates Ms. Gumbo; she is so mean." I agree. After we finish our conversation, I walk to my car and give her a ball that I used to play kickball with the kids in the community. "Would you give this to your kids?" I asked. She graciously accepts.

# The Isshinryuist: A Tale of Endurance

I have a long walk to get to the central office of the housing authority. There are no shoulders in St. Croix, so I always walk in the direction where I can see oncoming cars and I am ready to dive or run into the bushes at a moment's notice. The best part of walking is that I can think. I start emulating a tenth don who practices Gojo Ryu. His training methods are rigorous for any athlete. Especially his ki tiki ti designed to condition the body for strikes. I do condition my arms and legs with ko tiki ti, but I don't strike walls, boulders or hard, inanimate objects. If you haven't conditioned your hands in this manner, it will lead to excruciating pain. Some martial artists spend countless hours conditioning their knuckles, forearms and shins on hard objects. Others kick trees and break large chunks of ice with their feet, hands and heads, otherwise known as Tamashiwari (breaking of hard objects). The aforementioned don talks about how a person can train in martial arts from any location. His training encourages me to get my tonfas (weapon) out and I start doing complete circles with them in different directions. The tonfas return a guard position where they cover my entire forearm. The tonfas move quicker than usual because I am sweating heavily. I train with the tonfas until the bones in my forearms are so beat up that they don't want to take another miss-hit. It is difficult to swing the tonfas while walking. Finally, I arrive at the central office and from a distance I can see a few human figures; one is egg-shaped, which I know is going to be Mr. Swanson and as I get closer, my guess becomes fact.

# The Isshinryuist: A Tale of Endurance

When I walk by, Mr. Swanson asks, "Frenette what are you doing here?" I snap back, "I'm here to see Petunia." I go into the office and see all my friends. Petunia is acting sheepish because she knows that I was wronged. I see my dear friend Yvonne, who has a sparkle in her eye for me taking on this bully. Yvonne looks like Cindy Who from the Grinch movie, all grown up, dimples and all. I try not to get too close to any of these people because I don't want to cause them any type of duress after I leave, but everyone is coming up to me and talking to me as if to say, "Forget Swanson." I see Ms. Tatta, Ronnie and Isabella and we all talk as though nothing has changed. Mr. Swanson hates that I fit in with the employees. My co-workers ask me to mail them my book to their personal email address. They mention that they will love reading it and that it makes them feel as if they are living that moment; some passages make them laugh so hard that they spit out their coffee in the process. An anonymous reader writes, "Sensei Frenette, can you get me a picture of Mr. Swanson, he sounds like a real asshole?" I consider this reader to be the most intuitive of all of my anonymous readers. After walking back and forth between two doorways for some time, Mr. Swanson gathers the courage to tell me that I am not allowed on housing property. I respond by saying, "I go where I please." I have walked the most crime-ridden areas of Detroit, Hamtramck, New Orleans, Philadelphia, Atlantic City and many other large cities and now I am told that I am not allowed on public housing property. I haven't raised my voice, cursed or done anything wrong.

Living in the Virgin Islands was a great experience and equivalent to living in a foreign land. My desire to travel to Africa is fulfilled because there were so many African influences, including the desert, the tropical forest and the ocean. Women wear brightly colored clothing as in Africa and they can be seen carrying gallon jugs of milk on their head while carrying bags of groceries in each hand. The machete is commonly seen and prevalent on the island. I will always remember my time on St. Croix as well spent.

After it rains on St. Croix, my neighbor, Ron, prefers to let his car mats dry out on top of his vehicle rather than roll-up his windows. Before going to bed, I hear a constant beeping sound. I try to sleep in spite of it, but it's not possible. I get up and start to unplug various devices in my apartment. I also check my phones, but the beep persists. When I go into the bathroom, I hear the noise, but it now appears to be coming from the air conditioner outside so I decide to close the bathroom door and go back to bed. Then it occurs to me that the noise may be coming from Ron's apartment. I arrive at his place only to see smoke coming out from all four sides of his front door. I beat on the door repeatedly, to no avail. After a lengthy time I hear him fall against the door as he fumbles with the deadbolt for several minutes before opening the door. When he opens the door, smoke bellows out of his apartment and he's in a drunken stupor. He has the audacity to ask, "Why did you wake me up?" I spot two pans sitting on a propane stove set on high that are burning away. I go in and shut the stove off and scold him, "You need to quit doing those shots." I go back to my apartment. Still, he doesn't clear the smoke alarm, because of his intoxication. The smoke detector continues to beep. I go back into his apartment and rip the smoke detector off the wall. The next day I write "ASSHOLE" on an envelope and place it under his windshield wiper. My son says, "Dad, you have a way of making friends everywhere you go." I haven't spoken to Ron since and he makes himself scarce when he sees me pull up. On another occasion I hear Ron coming home, and the sound of heavy movements and objects being slammed around makes me think he's drunk again. I hear a loud thump. My guess is that he fell and hit his head on the countertop. I smile thinking, "Sleep alas."

# The Isshinryuist: A Tale of Endurance

I embark on a kayak ride to Buck Island which is five miles east of St. Croix. The tropical winds were at a steady twenty-five miles an hour and with gust reaching 35 miles which produce four-foot white caps. After bidding Jerry (Cabana Boy) farewell I realize that I don't have a life jacket. I turn back for a life jacket because I need and I want one. The water sprayed over the kayak stinging my face. I am certain that I am going to make it no matter what. I don't want to hear anyone say that I had to turn back. I paddle and paddle but it seems like I'm not making any progress because of the wind. I keep the kayak bow going straight into the waves reducing my chances of capsizing. I notice that after a short while the water turns black, which means it's really deep. This fact doesn't concern me because six-feet of water are more than enough for a person to drown in. Most people drown at the surface gasping for air. That said, I control my mind and I don't let it control me. I mark places that are next to me to monitor my progress. I stroke time and again and then I turn my head to check my progress. It seems as though no progress is made according to my benchmark. I come up with a plan to keep my kayak in forward motion. I give it thirty strokes as hard as I can and then I ten lighter strokes to let my arms recover a bit. This seems to work and I begin to move forward, but not much. Buck Island looks a long way away, but (five miles) I kept this pace up until I reach my destination. I won't reach inside the cooler for a drink because I don't want the kayak to go backwards. The way that I am bent-over in the kayak starts to cause some cramping because I am not used to sitting like a half-opened jack-knife for such a long time. I see boats in the distance and people are waving at me. They are probably wondering, "What is that nut doing out here with these type of waves." I don't take the time to wave back. The only distraction is a giant turtle that comes up out of the water. It is so large that at first I think it's a whale. The turtle is as large as a compact car and it surfaces only for a brief moment; it's about fifty feet away from me and has an orange tint to it. After it goes down, it never resurfaces.

My arms are burning as I press forward towards the island. It is amazing how long it takes to move just a few feet. I thought paddling would get easier when I was behind the island to help block the wind, but the waves were as ferocious as ever. As I get closer, I make something out in the distance. At first I see something tall, which turns out to be the mast of a sail boat. Afterwards, I notice movement on the beach which turns out to be people moving about the island. I am happy that I train as hard as I do because this was no easy task paddling in these conditions. My arms have been burning since I left. When I make it to the island, I'm so exhausted from paddling that I forget how hard the waves are hitting the beach. (The thought of training in the community room after paddling to Buck Island quickly fades.) As I get out of the kayak, a brutal wave picks up the kayak knocking me backwards and then dropping the kayak down on my foot. Without a whimper I finish pulling the kayak to shore. I drag it fifteen-feet up a small hill making sure the kayak doesn't slip back into the sea and leave me stranded on Buck Island. As I look at my foot, I start to feel intense pain. I watch as a lump on the top of my ankle grows to the size of an egg. Buck Island looks like any other undeveloped island. The only difference is the sand, which has a smooth and creamy texture because its granules are very fine.

# The Isshinryuist: A Tale of Endurance

There are three or four large boats taking tourists from St. Croix to Buck Island. A round trip fare is eighty dollars. There are a lot of people swimming and fighting the huge waves in the warm Caribbean Sea. The water is always inviting, and it is so warm, that I imagine steam being released from its surface. I talk with a tour-boat worker who tells me that she is impressed at the way I paddled against the wind and at the time it took me to get to Buck Island.

Kayaking is another way to cross-train for my martial arts, and one of the reasons that I embarked on this adventure. Plus, I want to snorkel with the barracudas, which are present in great numbers here. My foot throbs with every heartbeat. I spot a picnic table located in the shade. I lie on top of it and fall fast asleep. Later, while taking a swim, I notice a woman sitting in the water tinkering with her mask. A wave comes and engulfs her flipping her over as though she is doing a backward summersault. The water has her full attention. I go after her mask while her husband tries to pull her up off her back. But she is big, the size of Ms. Gumbo and we struggle to get her up. After we steady her, another wave hits and takes us to the sand. They thank me and I limp back to my kayak to head back to the Tamarind Reef Resort on St. Croix.

I find out the reefs and the Barracudas are on the other side of the Island and because of the waves and my aching foot, this adventure will have to wait. I have a long journey ahead of me to get back to St. Croix. The trip back is easier, but it takes a while. The hardest part is keeping the kayak straight while paddling to keep me from being tipped over from the large waves.

# The Isshinryuist: A Tale of Endurance

When I arrive at Tamarind Reef, I am so happy to get out of the half-opened jack-knife position and stand up straight. After putting the kayak away and returning the life jacket to the beach hut, Sonia, the attendant, notices my swollen foot and advices me to see a doctor. I spit on it and forget about it. I am making preparations to leave the island. My car is sailing to what I consider The Land of Milk and Honey, the United States. I had some great times and made some friendships here, but I am ready to leave. I enjoy eating organic food along with being presented with a variety of food choices that are within my price range, something that isn't possible on the island. The wildlife on the island is limited, especially with bird species. There are no chickadees, robins, warblers or bald eagles. The excitement is on the mainland, a place where one can enjoy ping-pong, roller-blading, racket-ball, etc. without experiencing the extreme heat of St. Croix.

# The Isshinryuist: A Tale of Endurance

Sonia

After living on St. Croix and staying at a place where I where I am so far away from everything it seems like a place someone would choose to hide from the law. I live amongst the mongooses, cacti, banana trees and lizards. There are so many mosquitoes here that I run from my car to get into my apartment, but I never succeed in avoiding a bite because they always get in. However, I am fortunate that I don't swell or itch from mosquito bites. My place looks like one of those motels fashioned after a strip mall, the kind you notice on the side of a foothill going through Kentucky. That has a permanent billboard erected on the property advertising their name and a continuous white vacancy sign written on plywood in large black lettering. Nevertheless, this place feels like the Hilton Hotel after having slept in a rental car for an extended period, but it soon loses its luster. Luckily, it has air conditioning, which is desperately needed on the desert side of the Island. To advance my Isshinryu training I walk up and down the mountains only stopping to do my katas and basics up on vertical grades of six or more. A vertical six on a highway has runaway truck ramps filled with sand in case a semi-truck loses its brakes. It doesn't take long to work up a good sweat. I start sweating as soon as I close my apartment door.

My new dojo is outside and absolutely beautiful. It overlooks the Caribbean Sea where its turquoise waves gently splash against the shoreline. The water is so clear that I can see the coral from the mountain tops while I watch the freighters go by in the distance. I don't believe a martial artist could have a more glamorous dojo to train. As I walk through the community where I work, some of the residents mention they have seen me training in the mountains.

# The Isshinryuist: A Tale of Endurance

I find a new place to live and it's a luxurious home where I am able to rent a room for $500 a month. It includes full access to everything, along with comfortable furniture. It sits on a couple of acres, has a pool, covered porches and a landscaped yard and a private bath and a separate entrance. Here is where I met Sonia and Tom (Sonia's boyfriend). I never met a person who talked as much as Tom. He doesn't even give Sonia (kayak attendant a chance to think, his sentences are continuous. It seems as if I am watching a show on Sixty Minutes where a man exploits a woman for her money. I am concerned for Sonia, but I know better than to get involved.

Tom has all the qualities of being a real, live gigolo. He's good looking, fit, romantic and is dating an older woman. His incessant talking forces me to wear ear plugs while I read. Generally, I am able to tune out most things, but not Tom. His worse quality is his unwillingness to shut the screen doors, giving mosquitoes free rein to get into the house. Dengue fever is prevalent on the Island and a "new batch" of mosquitoes carrying Dengue fever is being brought to the island on a regular basis from underdeveloped countries.

Sonia's son, Trey, came to the Island and stayed at the house for a week. He gives my Isshinryu, celebrity status. Before he came to the island, everyone thinks I'm just a fool working out incessantly, but they did give me credit for working out every evening and hitting the fitness trail.

# The Isshinryuist: A Tale of Endurance

Trey had been in the Army and was stationed in Afghanistan for most of his deployment, but he was released early on a medical after being injured by a road-side bomb, Improvised Explosive Device (IED). He trained as a sniper and most of his time was spent patrolling the remote mountains of Afghanistan. Trey appeared on a TV documentary. If you don't know much about snipers, there are three qualities that you must have: 1) Keep yourself in top physical condition, 2) Have the ability to do mathematical calculations and 3) Is pure genetics...you must have excellent eyesight. And this is what stops most people from ever becoming a sniper, their eyesight. Once a sniper, you must qualify each year to continue in this position. The sniper wears all the appropriate camouflage while the spotters look for the sniper in the field using binoculars. If the spotters find the sniper, the sniper is instantly disqualified from continuing in that position; no matter how long that person has held that position.

Trey recounts the time when he was qualifying to be a sniper and the spotters looked for him the entire day. He explains, "That he sneaks up on them from behind and is no more than a few yards from them." When someone yells out, "Has anyone seen Trey? We have been looking for him all day." Trey rises up behind him and says, "I am right here!"

Trey is about 6'2', blonde hair and cuts his hair close to a military style. He is thin, muscular, has sky blue eyes and is in his late twenties. He is well- mannered and doesn't drink anymore because of an experience he had at a bar thrashing a bouncer and a policeman. Somehow, he ended up pointing the officer's gun at his head with the officer begging for his life. The only reason he isn't in jail is because of his lawyer's defense tactic. He used Post Traumatic Stress Disorder (PTSD) as the cause of the incident. Trey and I connect immediately and I stay up late listening to his stories.

As we talk he wants to know more about Isshinryu. Usually, I don't let people know about my involvement in Isshinryu until they been in my circle for a while. Nevertheless, I explain to him how Isshinryu is a confluence from Gojo Ryu and Shorin Ryu which makes up Isshinryu. Because of this, I am able to slide back and forth between styles as needed for techniques. I can use Gojo Ryu for hard strikes and blocks or enter into Shorin-Ryu utilizing its soft strikes and blends for my techniques, while taking advantage of Isshinryu's style to fit natural body motions that are adapted for the human body by using neutral body stances. In Isshinryu, tension is your enemy, and when you feel tension, something is wrong with your technique. It is important to be aware of tension while doing kata; if you feel weak while doing kata it is because of two things: you haven't mastered the move or you are not working within your strength zones. The best way to describe this is: if your hand crosses the center part of your body, or you may be reaching too far, each will lessen the effectiveness of the technique. Remember, kata tells a story and it will reveal your level of attainment in the martial arts. Most people think that the belt color is the indicator of your achievement in the martial arts. When I want to get an idea of a person's commitment to the arts, I ask, "How long have you trained and who have you trained under?" It is the blood line that a karate-ka must be concerned with and this means his instructors' blood line (who he/she has trained under).

Trey is intrigued and wants to know more about bunkai (the application of kata) than kata. This isn't surprising usually the younger men are. I start by teaching Trey how to make a fist, Isshinryu 101. Afterwards, I start working on destroying his arms as he punches. I work using techniques from Gojo Ryu first and then I start extending his energy using Shorin-Ryu techniques. He is so impressed that he later tells Sonia that he has never seen martial arts taught in such a fashion.

Even Tom talked about training with me if he had more time. Tom and I become friends and this comes about after his scooter breaks down. He didn't ask Sonia to drive him all over the island. He just grabs his backpack and starts walking until his chariot is fixed, which takes two weeks. Before leaving the island, I leave most of my belongings to Tom, especially, my prized possessions, which consist of expensive fins, my spear with three prongs and a huge rubber band attached to it to help propel it through the water quickly, my mask and a machete. I killed a fish with the spear and I felt bad afterwards for shortening his life. This is one of the reasons I have never been a good hunter, plus, I don't have the skills for it. Tom enjoyed our friendship because he has someone else to talk to, while I focused on my listening skills. After saying goodbye to the Virgin Islands I arrived in Miami and stay with friends while I wait for my car, which is being shipped over.

## JD

JD is one of the smartest men I have ever met. He has a Juries Doctorate Degree and is a CPA. He considers himself a professional test-taker. He explains that the CPA test is harder to pass than the bar exam. I have found out through friends close to JD that he is able to hide huge sums of money overseas where no one would ever be able to find it. I think he downplays his abilities. He is an exceptional tennis player, one whom I have never even come close to beating. I have learned to never doubt his knowledge on politics and current events because his knowledge runs deep in those subjects.

JD's father is credited with bringing up the IQ of America by removing the lead from gasoline. Trish, his wife, is an MD who has tied her practice closely with holistic medicine and is licensed to practice medicine in two states and gives lectures worldwide.

I met JD and Trish the first week I moved to Asheville. I have worked for them and have been friends with them ever since. I make sure to visit them when they come to Asheville. I ask JD if I can stay at his place in Miami until my car arrives. I don't like to stay anywhere for free. JD is excited to have me stay with him and I know I will be treated like a king. JD and I finish up projects around his house and catch up on our friendship. I don't charge for my services; I'm just happy to have a place to stay until my car arrives. My main concern is that my car isn't held up at the Mona Passage, a turbulent part of the sea that lies between the islands of Hispaniola and Puerto Rico.

# The Isshinryuist: A Tale of Endurance

After arriving in Miami, JD notifies me that we are to meet Trish at one of the five-star restaurants they frequent. Once there, I give Trish a big hug and we have an excellent dinner. During dinner I tell them that I feel like Nelson Mandela eating his first meal after being released from prison. Nearly eight months have gone by since I have savored a fine meal such as this. The food on St Croix is expensive and the choices are very limited. At dinner we exchange stories and they ask me about my trip. I tell them that it was an adventure that I will never forget and that I made a lot of friends, especially, at St. Croix Housing. I tell them that the only reason people live on the Island is to feed the bugs, because, if there weren't any people to bite, there wouldn't be any bugs. I mention that St. Croix is hotter than anywhere I have ever been and that my car air conditioner ran full blast during the entire length of my stay. After arriving at JD's house he shows me my room, which looks like a suite. Then he gives me the alarm codes plus the keys to everything and offers me his car; however, I see a bike and ask if I can use that instead.

The two treasures that I bring back from the island is my friendship with Sonia and Tom whom I lived with for three months, and The Jolt, a hand-held bug zapper made in Africa. I buy four of the ingenious inventions. One is for JB, who does not think much of it until he sees it work and exclaims, "This is the best present I have ever received." I give one to my cousin; one is for me and the other one is for my son. This is all I can carry. I was hard to part without my fins, mask and spear as we had some unforgettable adventures together in the Caribbean Sea. It amazed me to see how many people on the Island cannot swim or have never gone to the other side of the Island. To live in same location your entire life is like reading the same chapter over and over again.

THE END

I don't know what I would have done without Isshinryu in my life. It has been with me through all the low and high points of my life. Isshinryu has stayed while many women have gone. Yes, I truly love Isshinryu. My last thoughts that I would like to leave my readers and I have many because I am an avid reader. "No matter how dark the tunnel is, there will always be light at the end of it." Roald Amundsen (Founder of the South Pole).

Works Cited

Paderewski, Ignacy Jan. "If I miss one day of practice.....
Quote Paderewsi, Ignacy Jan. "Collection of Famous and
Popular Quotes." <i>Iz Quotes</i>. N.p., n.d. Web. 09 Nov.
2015.